THE MARY ROSE MUSEUM

The Mary Rose Museum is the eighth in a series of books which describe an entirely new attitude toward architecture and building. The books are intended to provide a complete working alternative to our present ideas about architecture, building, and planning — an alternative which will, we hope, gradually replace current ideas and practices.

Volume 1   THE TIMELESS WAY OF BUILDING
Volume 2   A PATTERN LANGUAGE
Volume 3   THE OREGON EXPERIMENT
Volume 4   THE LINZ CAFE
Volume 5   THE PRODUCTION OF HOUSES
Volume 6   A NEW THEORY OF URBAN DESIGN
Volume 7   A FORESHADOWING OF 21ST CENTURY ART:
              THE COLOR AND GEOMETRY OF VERY
              EARLY TURKISH CARPETS
Volume 8   THE MARY ROSE MUSEUM

Future volumes now in preparation include

Volume 9   THE NATURE OF ORDER
Volume 10   SKETCHES OF A NEW ARCHITECTURE
Volume 11   BATTLE: THE STORY OF A HISTORIC CLASH
               BETWEEN WORLD SYSTEM A AND WORLD SYSTEM B
Volume 12   THE PRECIOUS JEWEL

The authors gratefully acknowledge the help of the with the following staff and consultants, who worked throughout the project, and whose work is reflected in this book: John Hewitt, Annie Der Bedrossian, James Maguire, Saul Pichardo, Noor Awan, Ingrid King, Mike Campbell, Paul Frick, Alan Baxter, Randy Schmidt, Eleni Coromvli, Kleoniki Tsotropoulou, Ora Hathaway, Charles Han, David Sidebotham, and Katalin Bende. We want to thank, especially, Annie Der Bedrossian, whose beautiful drawings appear on pages 6, 18–21, 50, and 104–5; and John Hewitt whose support throughout has been of an extraordinary nature.

THE
MARY ROSE
MUSEUM

Christopher Alexander, Chief Architect
Gary Black, Chief Engineer
Miyoko Tsutsui

with thanks for the continued support and encouragement of
Brian Hanson
Director of The Prince of Wales's Institute of Architecture

NEW YORK • OXFORD
OXFORD UNIVERSITY PRESS

1995

THIS VOLUME HAS BEEN PUBLISHED

IN PART

WITH THE HOPE THAT IT WILL CONTINUE TO STIMULATE SUPPORT FOR

CONSTRUCTION OF THE MARY ROSE MUSEUM

Published by Oxford University Press, Inc., 200 Madison Avenue, New York, New York 10016. Oxford is a registered trademark of Oxford University Press. All rights reserved. No part of this publication can be reproduced, stored in a retrieval system, or transmitted, in any form or by any means, electronic, mechanical, photocopying, recording, or otherwise, without the prior permission of Oxford University Press.

Library of Congress Cataloging-in-Publication Data:
Alexander, Christopher. The Mary Rose Museum / Center for
Environmental Structure :
Christopher Alexander, Gary Black, Miyoko Tsutsui,
with the following staff and consultants, John Hewitt . . . [et al.].
p. cm. — (Center for Environmental Structure Series ; v. 8).
ISBN 0-19-521017-4.
1. Mary Rose Museum. 2. Mary Rose (Ship). 3. Naval Museums—
England—Portsmouth. I. Black, Gary. II. Tsutsui, Miyoko.
III. Center for Environmental Structure. IV. Title.
V13.G72P673 1994.
387′.0074′422792—dc20   93-18221

Manufactured in Japan by Dai Nippon Printing Co., Ltd.

© 1995
CENTER FOR ENVIRONMENTAL STRUCTURE
BERKELEY, CALIFORNIA

DEDICATED

TO HIS ROYAL HIGHNESS THE PRINCE OF WALES

IN RECOGNITION OF HIS SUPPORT FOR THE WORLD-WIDE MOVEMENT

TO CREATE A BETTER ARCHITECTURE

AND TO ENCOURAGE HIM TO CONTINUE

IN THESE ENDEAVORS

IN SPITE OF RESISTANCE AND OPPOSITION

FOR THE BENEFIT OF PEOPLE EVERYWHERE

South view with HMS Victory *and Victory Arena*

CONTENTS

BACKGROUND: THE PORTSMOUTH DOCKYARD
AND THE *MARY ROSE*   page 9

PROLOGUE   page 13

I. THE FIRST VISION   page 25

II. EARLY MODELS AND SKETCHES   page 33

III. THE FIRST DESIGN: REALIZING THE VISION   page 47

IV. ACHIEVING A GREAT BUILDING — CONSTRUCTION PROCESS
AND COST CONTROL   page 79

V. SKETCHES OF A SECOND DESIGN   page 101

EPILOGUE: THE MEANING OF THE MARY ROSE MUSEUM   page 123

THE PORTSMOUTH
DOCKYARD AND THE
MARY ROSE

Painting of the Mary Rose *from the Anthony Roll, c. 1546*

Victory Gate: the entrance to the Dockyard

The *Mary Rose* was one of Henry VIII's biggest and most important warships. It was built in the Portsmouth Dockyard, launched in 1510, and sailed for 35 years. In 1545, during a lull in a battle with the French fleet, it suddenly and unaccountably

The mast pond: Boathouse #6 in the background

Overview of the Portsmouth Dockyard

sank, in calm seas, one mile offshore. Henry VIII himself was watching and saw his ship go down, with 700 men on board. Fewer than three dozen survived.

The ship was found again in 1977, after twelve years of search, by Alexander McKee and Margaret Rule.[1] It was brought to the surface by Margaret Rule in 1982, and now lies in dry dock #3 in the Royal Naval Dockyard, Portsmouth, only a few feet from the place where it was built, and just over a mile from where it sank. Since

An early view of the Portsmouth Dockyard, c. 1717

1 Alexander McKee, a journalist and amateur diver, was the organizer of the first dives to find the *Mary Rose* in 1965. Margaret Rule, an archeologist who accompanied McKee on the first dives, is now archeological director of the *Mary Rose* and of the museum.

The Royal Naval Museum and other buildings between Victory Gate and the Mary Rose Museum

1982 the ship has been protected by a temporary tent-like structure. In 1989 the dry dock was sealed by a permanent dam, with the *Mary Rose* inside.

The need to create a permanent museum to house the ship has now become evident. This permanent Museum must be built over the existing dock, spanning it completely, since the dry dock itself is a historic structure which cannot be permitted to take any significant loads. The new Museum must function as a workshop to house the continuing stabilization and reconstruction of the ship until about 2020, and must then be capable of transition to its long-term role as the permanent home for the ship.

In addition, the Museum must play a key role in the architecture of the historic Portsmouth Dockyard: the area which has now become known as the Heritage Area. It must, somehow, in standing next to HMS *Victory*, enhance rather than detract from the magnificent spectacle of Nelson's flagship. It must also intensify the harmonious relationships of the historic brick buildings all around; consolidate the emotional core of the historic Dockyard; and be a work of modern engineering.

PROLOGUE

A BUILDING WORTHY OF THE *MARY ROSE* AND OF THE PORTSMOUTH DOCKYARD

In December 1990, the Prince of Wales asked me to see him on some general architectural matters. During the discussion, he pointed to a set of drawings of a design for the new Mary Rose Museum which had been made for a developer in the hope of attracting the Mary Rose Trust and securing the building commission. In his capacity as President of the Mary Rose Trust, His Royal Highness was deeply disappointed by the drawings which showed a crude and over-simplified glass and steel box that appeared quite unfitting for a museum destined to hold Henry VIII's great ship *Mary Rose*. It was also strikingly at odds with the subtle harmony of the Portsmouth Dockyard.

He turned and asked me what I might be able to do to help. I said that I was prepared to do whatever he thought necessary. In the course of the discussion which followed, as he and Brian Hanson and I were studying the glass and steel box drawings together, he took out a pencil and very rapidly sketched on the back of one of the drawings, a small drawing only two or three inches across, with the comment "Couldn't we do something like this."

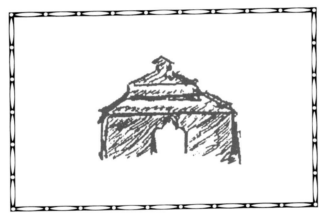

A shaded version of the sketch drawn by the Prince of Wales
at about half the size he drew it

The Prince of Wales's drawing was made, originally, as a way of explaining what he hoped for. It was an inspiration for the building.[2]

The actual design, of course, evolved over many months, after much discussion and deliberation with the Mary Rose Trust and after consideration of functional, structural, and site-planning requirements. However, the design was formulated within the framework of the feeling and inspiration of this sketch, and so when one compares the original sketch with the final product there is a distinct resemblance. At the time the Prince made the sketch he was intimately familiar with the Portsmouth Dockyard and with the *Mary Rose*. The sketch was, in effect, a thumbnail embodiment of what a

2 Reproductions of the Prince's sketch have appeared previously in other publications, including the London newspaper THE MAIL ON SUNDAY, Sunday, March 14, 1993 and the British architectural journal BUILDING DESIGN, March 19, 1993.

"right" architecture for that ship and that place might look like. The resemblance of the actual building, as we designed it, to this original sketch, comes about, not because he was President of the Mary Rose Trust, or because we sought to follow him too closely, but—I believe—because the actual building as we designed it, was generated from the same underlying principles as the sketch itself. Both forms come from a shared feeling about the true meaning and purpose of architecture, and from a shared feeling of what these lead to, on that site in Portsmouth, for the Mary Rose Museum.

The sketch has simple and valuable qualities. It is symmetrical. It forms a clear center which is felt "as" a center. It has a hierarchy of levels in it. Its forms reflect human feeling. Even, in rudimentary form, there is some sense of a possible arched structure of a building—all visible already in these few pencil strokes.

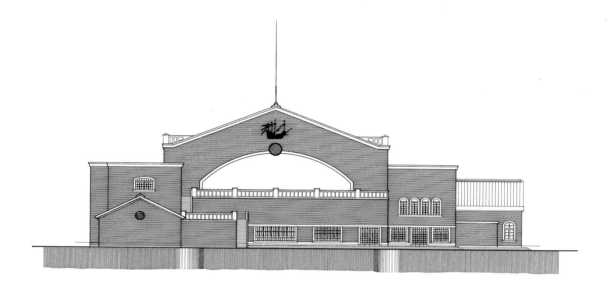

West view of the Museum, from the water

So this sketch, and our building, show a direction that may be needed to pull our present-day architecture away from the mid–twentieth century forms it has had, and towards new forms of the 21st century, in which human feeling comes first.

After further discussion in the days following the Prince of Wales's request, I was invited by other officers of the Mary Rose Trust to visit the ship in Portsmouth, and to have discussions with Margaret Rule, chief archaeologist of the *Mary Rose*, and other Trustees. Not long afterwards the Mary Rose Trust formally commissioned the Center for Environmental Structure to design the Museum.

We worked intermittently, for about eighteen months. However, in July 1992, before our work was finished, the fate of the Museum came into serious question. The shipping company which had originally put up the money for architectural fees, and which had intended to pay £5 million towards the building shell, withdrew their funds from the Dockyard. This made immediate construction of the new museum impossible, and prompted the Mary Rose Trust to consider various alternative low budget plans to protect the ship with temporary measures while conservation proceeds. Most of these temporary plans seem to require construction funds ranging from £350,000 to £2,000,000.

A permanent museum will be built for the *Mary Rose*, on this site, at a later date, once funds for the permanent Museum become available. It is possible to construct the Museum as we show it in this book, either in total, or incrementally, over the existing tent, without in any way interrupting the conservation program. Further, and what is highly significant, the first phase of the permanent Museum can be built for no more than about £2 million, as described on pages 118–122, thereby alleviating or possibly eliminating the need to re-clad the existing tent, and thus avoiding waste of donor funds on a temporary building which must be torn down after thirty years to make way for a new one. This would also rapidly replace the current tent, which is not harmonious with HMS *Victory*, and which should not be allowed to stand longer than absolutely necessary.

What follows is a description of the outline of the Museum which we have designed for the *Mary Rose*. It includes the original vision which inspired the building, the first design, and the second design, together with analysis of the major technical issues, centering above all on cost, engineering, and the practical framework needed to make the construction possible.

We hope that these materials, as they appear in this book, will inspire friends of the *Mary Rose*, all over the world, to support the construction of a new and permanent museum. It is, thus, our hope that this book, showing the evolution of the design with the Mary Rose Trust, will itself play a role in the further development of the project during the next months and years.

The Mary Rose Museum is potentially one of the most important buildings to be built in England in this decade. We believe that the importance of the building, to the Dockyard, to the people of Portsmouth, and to the visitors who come in thousands to see HMS *Victory* and *Mary Rose* each year, must not be underestimated. What is needed to house it is a sober building which is harmonious with the Dockyard, a building which will inspire generations of museum visitors.

One of the most important things at stake in this building concerns the vision of a new architecture, humane in feeling, profound in meaning, *of* the 21st century, yet consistent with the thousand-year-old tradition of architecture. It is a vision which has enormous importance not only for people in England but for people all over the world. This vision, towards which my colleagues and I have struggled for many years, is the clue to a humane life, and decent society, and a humane experience of ordinary human feeling in our daily lives.

This is the temporary tent structure which the new museum will replace

It should also be said that this vision of a new architecture in a new world is at the core of the Prince of Wales's recently founded Institute of Architecture. The Institute was founded in London, in 1992, as an institution for teaching architecture and as an organization which promotes the aims of this new architecture in practical building projects and experiments. From the first days of the Institute and in my role as a founding member of the Academic Board, I considered the Mary Rose Museum as a vitally important project, because of its public nature, and because of the promise it holds as a step towards that future which the Institute supports.

The changed concept of design, a change of attitude from purely technical and commercial issues of flexibility and exhibition management (typical of a "box" type of museum), towards fundamental human needs and feelings, is difficult to grasp in the context of present-day 20th century architecture. It is not consistent with the frame of mind which has created our recently built urban landscape of office buildings and commercial developments. The new forms of construction management which are needed to allow making such a building, by careful control of cost and design while the building is being built, and by greater concentration on craft, are all unfamiliar.

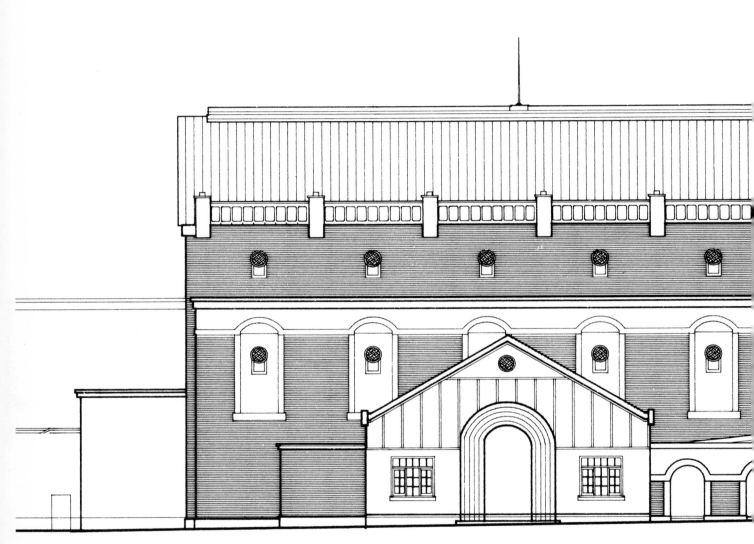

The second design: south elevation

That is where the breakdown in our civilization has occurred. The impetus towards common sense and feeling in the construction of the environment has been trampled, again and again, by market and business considerations which have no deep connection at all to human need or human aspirations, or to human spirituality. Within such a social atmosphere King's College chapel or the magnificent abbey barn at Great Cox-

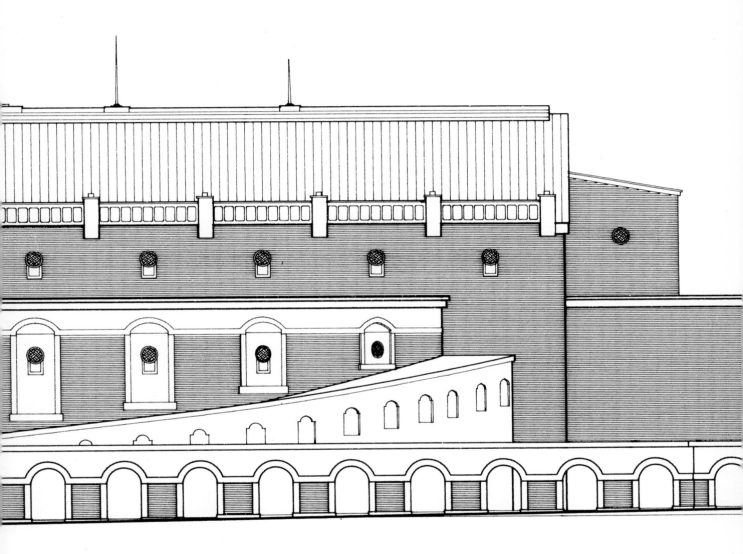

well in Berkshire could never have been built. The only hope for a future in which feeling and human significance once again mark and touch our world — and our buildings — is a different way of thinking which must first be introduced successfully in a few landmark projects. Then, once that has been accomplished, there is a chance it will prevail.

The first design: view of HMS Victory *and main entrance*

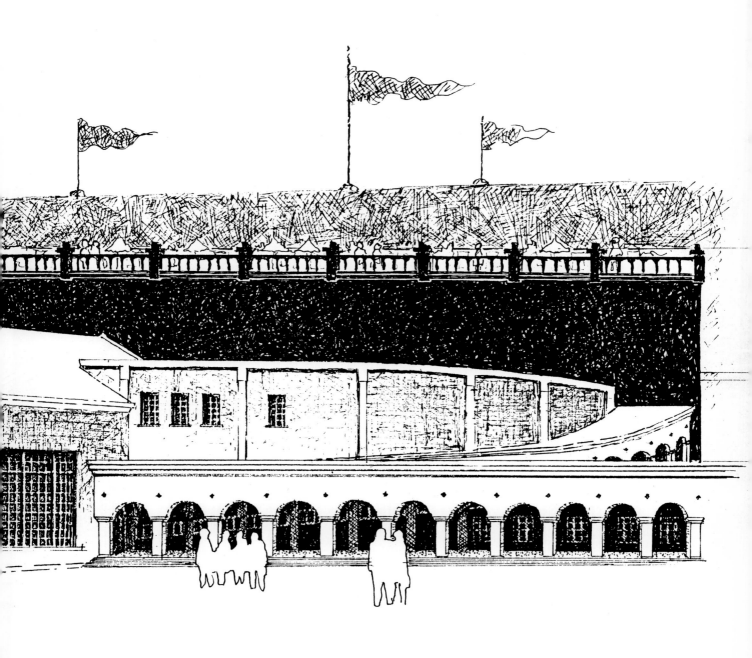

The first design: view from the west

In order to move towards this vision of a new and better world, in which the feelings of ordinary people are respected in every stone, brick, window, bench, path, street and flowerbed, it is necessary that all the people who take part in projects of this kind have a certain amount of courage. It requires courage to help solve the problems which are inherent in our present forms of architecture and construction management as they exist in society today.

Courage is essential. During the first phase of the Mary Rose Museum project, certain problems occurred because these matters were misunderstood. When fundamental changes in design are coupled with fundamental changes in the conception of space, changes in the conception of building, and—on top of that—with changes in engineering, changes in money management and changes in construction management, it is very easy for the situation to be misunderstood. People may then disagree because the profound and simple concepts that are needed to get buildings right are unexpected, perhaps even frightening, insofar as they turn away from the familiar. But these things need not be frightening. They are, at root, practical and sound. The practical embodiment of a society in which human values are given their proper weight, always lies in an architecture where buildings too give human values and matters of human spirit their proper weight. What is involved, in the construction of the Mary Rose Museum, as we hope to see it built, is potentially just such a turning point. It requires a new conception of human spirit, coupled with technology, that could ultimately—I believe—represent a turning point in modern society.

Christopher Alexander
Chief Architect

CHAPTER ONE

THE FIRST VISION

A MUSEUM BUILDING AND PUBLIC SQUARE TO BE BUILT IN THE
ROYAL NAVAL DOCKYARD, PORTSMOUTH, OVER DRY DOCK #3,
TO HOUSE KING HENRY VIII'S SHIP THE *MARY ROSE*

The Mary Rose Museum is to house one of the greatest naval archaeological finds of all time—the warship *Mary Rose*. The building has to create the setting in which to display a diamond.

It is to be a place for people—fresh and beyond the sterile and tiring atmosphere associated with most museums. It is to be a place where people can be truly comfortable, where they can sit and think in a café, enjoy themselves, enjoy the Dockyard. And it is to be a memorial to the 700 men who lost their lives on that day in 1545 when the *Mary Rose* sank just a mile offshore while Henry VIII was watching—a building fitting for the historical Dockyard, for the residents of Portsmouth, and for the larger community of England.

What follows is a word-picture which embodies our original vision of the new Museum, as it was first written in February 1991. This word-picture is no longer entirely accurate: the Museum as we now envision it does not follow this picture detail by detail; indeed certain elements of this picture have since been modified at the request of the chief archaeologist, Margaret Rule. However, the picture is printed here as it was written in early 1991, because it remains—from the point of view of feeling and vision—the most accurate picture which we have constructed.

THE MUSEUM FROM A DISTANCE

As you come around the bow of HMS *Victory* from the south, the Mary Rose Museum stands to the north, directly ahead. The long nave of the ship hall rises high, with the *Mary Rose*'s four masts rising from it. The volume of the nave is 80 meters long, and about 21 meters high. The masts rise to perhaps 30 meters. Although the building is imposing, it is also somber and straightforward, reflecting the atmosphere of the Dockyard. This somberness is reflected in dark materials and in a sparseness and simplicity of line.

Visible in the upper part near the roof are windows of colored glass, in which emblems from the *Mary Rose*, and flags and banners are depicted. One sees these windows from the outside—the sun glistens on them, and shines on the glass. At night especially, the banners and emblems glow darkly.

In front of the nave, to the left-hand end of its long side, is the entrance to the building. The entrance rises up high, but without competing with the march of the roofs and masts of the building behind it.

From the entrance, going up and off to the right, a long colonnaded ramp rises gently towards the right-hand end—the eastern end—of the *Mary Rose* nave.

THE VICTORY ARENA: A SMALL PUBLIC SQUARE BETWEEN THE *MARY ROSE* AND HMS *VICTORY*

In the space between the *Victory* and the Mary Rose Mu-

seum is a roughly square open space. This square, filled with seats, cobblestones, and paving, is really itself a main building, almost as important as the Museum itself. It is a forecourt to the *Mary Rose*, and a forecourt to the *Victory*. It plays a key role in the layout, since it is a focal point in the Dockyard.

The layout of this square is plain, made of straight lines and simple shapes. It is consistent in feeling with the historical Dockyard buildings and their plain arrangement.

In summer weather this square is filled with people, some eating, some simply enjoying the sun. There are seats there, benches in the shade where people may lie down, rest, sit, children can play, and families can relax between visits to the two great ships.

There are also possibilities for informal gatherings and performances: one can imagine midsummer concerts there, and other informal performances. The space is arranged so that as many as 300 people can sit there to enjoy a concert.

THE SEATS AROUND THE SQUARE

Victory Arena is bounded on two sides (south and east) by small buildings with a wide colonnade. An iron railing that forms the back of the colonnade separates it from the security area of the Dockyard.

The third side of the square, which is the front and entrance of the Mary Rose Museum, is also approached by a wide colonnade. The fourth side (west) is formed by HMS *Victory*.

In the middle of the arena is a formal center, a brick and stone meeting place with benches, partly secluded, partly shaded, partly in full sunshine.

THE MEMORIAL CHAPEL AND MEMORIAL WALK

On the east side of the square, opening off the colonnade, is a tiny memorial chapel no more than a few square feet in size. This chapel is made in remembrance of the 700 men who died in the *Mary Rose*; it is dedicated to those who have no known grave other than the sea.

The part of the colonnade leading to this chapel is the Memorial Walk.

Stone tablets commemorating the 700 men are placed along the wall which forms the back side of the colonnade. One passes these tablets in approaching the Mary Rose Museum. The tablets are carved in low relief and show the dress of archers and sailors of the time.

ENTRANCE AND PROCESSION TO THE INTERIOR

As you approach the Museum, whether from the square or from the Memorial Walk, you arrive at a major entrance building, which stands high, to the west end of the building's south face.

Inside this entrance, still at ground level, you see a miniature of the *Mary Rose*: the painting from the Anthony Roll, at actual size, on a parchment.[3]

You then begin to move up a colonnaded ramp which leads to the right. Along this ramp you visit further aspects of Tudor history, in preparation for the shipwreck. You see images of the battle, of the gun battles typical of the time, the ships which were involved—the history of the time, in which the fighting between French and English was continuing.

At the top of the ramp you pass through the Museum and arrive at an outdoor balcony on the north side. The balcony looks down into dry dock #4. As you stand there, looking at dock #4, you grasp the idea and shape of a dry dock, with the complete dock laid out beneath you. It is the clear vista of this dock that prepares the visitor for what will soon be experienced inside the Mary Rose Museum.

From the balcony you go into a film theater where you see a twelve-minute film of the raising of the *Mary Rose*. After the film you are left with your thoughts, in darkness, while you collect yourself.

You then move down, in a lift, into the bowels of the earth, to a level about five meters below the ground. You are now in the very heart of dry dock #3.

ENTERING FROM UNDERWATER

You now pass into an exhibit where you are literally underwater. For the visitor the experience of diving is recreated, so that you pass through seawater, to enter the space where the *Mary Rose* herself is seen for the first time.

After going through this underwater experience, you enter the chasm of the nave.

---

3 The Anthony Roll is a hand-drawn parchment from the year 1546 listing all the ships belonging to Henry VIII. The parchment is in the Library of Magdalene College, Cambridge.

INTERIOR OF THE NAVE

Physically you now pass through a tunnel in the back of the dock, and come out inside the dock about mid-level. You are at this moment on a stone platform, which has stone walkways to the left and to the right running the length of the dock. As you look around, you are aware that you are now inside — and within — a dry dock similar to dock #4. The stone walls are all around you. You are walking on stone. You are next to the stone walls. The hull of the ship looms above you.

High above, the great curved trusses of the ship hall loom in the mist.

Water is pouring off the hull. Mist and cold and wetness are all around. (If it were possible this would be desirable even after 2020, after conservation is completed, since it contributes to the atmosphere of the ship.)

The almost ghostly experience of seeing the *Mary Rose* itself, wet, glistening, and in the mists of the cold interior, the fact that it lay underwater for four hundred years.

BEGINNING TO GRASP THE NATURE OF THE SHIP

You now move forward in the dock, towards the *Mary Rose*. You approach platforms which allow you to get close to the ship itself.

Off to the left there are escalators and stairs which lead to an interior pageant area, a building within a building, where flags are flying, and warmth and light are visible, gleaming in the darkness.

You pass from the dock, up stairs, or escalators, or ramp, or lift, to the part of the museum building on the south of the nave. Here you dwell again, on the beauty of the original ship.

THE PAGEANT OF THE MUSEUM

The pageantry of the time (expressed in the beautiful miniature from the Anthony Roll), the beautiful and inspiring color and flags, the extraordinary power of the guns, the dress, materials, belongings, are now woven together in a splendid interior. The interior is black, gold, and red, with touches of other color among the red and gold, that conveys in literal terms the character of this ship in the time and presence of King Henry VIII.

Inside the building there are all kinds of displays — artifacts from the actual ship, reconstructions of interiors like the barber-surgeon's cabin, experiments which show guns, bows, and related items, working or partially working, music, musical instruments, dress, clothes-making and so on.

The individual displays are connected by a series of bridges and scaffolding that moves away from the pageant, to hover in space in the black void of the *Mary Rose* nave. At the end of each of these bridges there is a small platform that literally hangs in the void, at some position near the ship — in two places it actually passes within the space and volume of the ship itself.

THE SHIP IN THE DOCK

The wooden scaffold mid-air structure surrounds the ship at waterline level, and allows you to approach the ship at five different points.

The first approach is to the starboard side. You are at this moment standing high in the interior of the nave, approaching the ship from the stern, looking down the length of the hull. This scaffold is curved, following the curved line of the hull. As you walk along it, you can touch the outside timbers, and you can also see in through the open gun ports.

The second approach is high above the ship, looking down the starboard from the stern. From this position you are also able to see the stern of the ship rather close to you, with a full view of the sterncastle.

The third approach is from the port side, amidships, at the level of the main deck, looking at the barber-surgeon's cabin to the left and the carpenter's cabin to the right.

The fourth approach is to the main gun deck, at M4 and M5 positions.[4] Here the emphasis is on the guns themselves. They are on display in the neighboring gallery in the place where access to the ship occurs.

The fifth approach is low, at the hold level, amidships, where you see the stepping of the mast and storage arrays.

The ship itself is enclosed in a curtain of some kind — it may be an air curtain — separating the

---

4 The technical numbering system used by the archaeologists for different portions of the hull frame.

immediate atmosphere around the ship from the visitor during the conservation period.

Each of the bridges which hover out in space is supported on a half-arch cantilevered brace. From inside the nave you see these braces as beautiful and lace-like structures.

The main experience of the exhibit consists of visitors going back and forth between the beautiful items in the pageant building, and the actual places in the hull of the ship, so that one gradually builds up a picture of the living ship, as it was with its full complement, in 1545.

The idea is that you see not only the dead, glistening hull and timbers of the ship itself, but by the time you have been through all this, you feel as though you have seen the living sixteenth-century ship, as it was, in 1545.

EXHIBITS AND RECONSTRUCTIONS OF THE MARY ROSE

The pageant part of the Museum, in the south building, contains a series of small low-ceilinged rooms separated by walls and columns, where the columns, beams, and walls are "illuminated" by paintwork similar to that visible in a sixteenth-century miniature. The spaces are small, and passage from space to space is exciting and pleasant.

The whole feeling in this section is similar to the feeling of sixteenth-century England, in scale, color, space, and detail.

Inside, the exhibits themselves are in small groups. Each

one has explanations in sound, film, and written word. In as many cases as possible there is a way of experiencing and touching and manipulating the things, so that you actually experience them, not only look at them through a glass case.

Some of the exhibits are complete reconstructions like the barber-surgeon's cabin.

Others are experiments where, for instance, you can flex a bow, or load a breech-loaded gun.

Others involve participation of other immediate kinds, in painting, weaving, listening to or playing music.

Yet other examples: Exhibits where you can buy food and drink of the period; stowage of barrels, cooking. These exhibits are linked to the orlop deck.[5]

Sailing and navigation are on display high up — a place from which the lines of the ship can be appreciated, and where talk of masts and rigging is appropriate.

Exhibits showing social material and leisure. This display incorporates sound, light, texture and movement. What was it like between decks when the men weren't fighting? The Museum has good domestic and social material which requires low light to preserve it. The feeling of low light recreates the atmosphere which really did exist in the decks of the Mary Rose at the time it sailed.

The men: their health and stature. Putting flesh on the bones of history. Many of the men were carefully selected and of fine physique. They were not social dropouts press-ganged

from the nearest pub. The exhibits contain data on physique and general health and some new evidence about bone deformation caused by occupational stress.

How the ship was sailed and navigated. This can be linked to the great voyages of discovery and exploration.

War at sea. The weapons and military equipment. Here the visitor will have a full-scale experience. Light will be used to paint the scene. Temperature and air movement (cold, fresh air through gratings and gunports) plus movement of the decks implied by lighting rather than induced by complicated mechanics, can all help. This experience must lead the visitor to a good view of the main gun-deck of the ship itself.

Each time, after one of these experiences, you can pass along the suspended scaffold, and reach some point within the Mary Rose itself where this particular activity actually happened. So you visualize the two combined: a spot in the physical ship as it now is in the dock; the reconstructed detail you have seen in the Museum gallery; and the bridge connecting the two in space, tying together your knowledge of the reconstruction, linking the two.

ONE-FIFTH FULL-SIZE WORKING MODEL OF THE MARY ROSE

When it comes time to leave the pageant area there is a surprise in store.

As you pass from the red and gold Tudor rooms of this

5 The lowest main deck in the ship.

part of the Museum, you find your way to an enclosed building. As you enter this building you find yourself in a wind tunnel which contains a one-fifth full-size working model of the *Mary Rose* actually sailing on real water.

The model ship is huge, more than 7 meters long, with masts nearly 10 meters high, and under full sail, all paintwork intact, flags flying. The waves are dashing; wind is howling. Wind is created by enormous fans, water moving to counteract the movement of the ship, as on a treadmill. The model of the *Mary Rose* is radio-controlled.

In this place you see and feel the full impact of the ship as it once was. You experience the actual behavior of the ship under a variety of wind conditions and maneuvers. It shows us, as nearly as possible, what it was actually like to see the *Mary Rose* itself, under sail, four hundred and fifty years ago.

LEAVING THE MUSEUM

As you leave the Museum you pass through another smaller hall where a giant image of the ship, similar in feeling to the Anthony Roll miniature, is projected, moving, so that you experience the full color, drama, movement of the man-of-war at sea, with all sails set and all flags and pennants flying.

This is your last glimpse of the *Mary Rose*, as you pass through the darkness of the dark cold ship, and back again to this image of the living ship, with sound, color, and motion.

MUSEUM SHOP

On your way back to Victory Arena you pass through a large Museum shop, in which many kinds of items connected with the *Mary Rose* and its story can be bought.

THE MUSEUM RESTAURANT

From the outside of the Museum, or from the inside, you can approach the restaurant. It is in the roof space above the ship hall. This restaurant is high above the harbor, a long narrow hall, with beautiful windows looking over the Dockyard and the water.

The restaurant has outdoor terraces which open from the restaurant itself. These terraces, sheltered from the wind, have beautiful views over the harbor. In summer, the terrace which faces south will have sunshine and shade from hanging vines.

You reach the restaurant by lift, directly from the museum entrance. This lift is open, and gives access to the restaurant even when the Museum is closed.

The glowing, colored windows, visible from the outside, which have heraldry and emblems from the *Mary Rose*, are the upper windows of the restaurant.

As you leave the Museum you walk out to a sunny terrace on the water. This terrace, which looks out into the inner basin of Portsmouth Harbor, is open in summer, glazed in winter.

Boat tours leave from this quay, to take you out around HMS *Warrior*[6] and then back towards the Museum with its

great arch visible and above it the masts of the *Mary Rose*.

At the water's edge is a smaller museum café. It is a place which allows leisure, and comfort. Waiters are not rushing you out of your place. There is a commitment from the restaurant to leave you for as long as you like, sitting and enjoying the memory of what you have seen.

WORKSHOPS AND OFFICES

On the north side of the nave there is a large variety of offices and workshops devoted to the reconstruction of the ship and its artifacts. Here laboratory experiments concerned with the project are carried out.

EXTERIOR MATERIALS AND COLOR

The color of the Museum is an overall combination of black, pink, red, light grey, and white. It is reminiscent of the colors which appear in the portrait of Henry VIII's sister, Mary Rose herself, black clothes, red accents, white and grey touches.[7]

These colors are realized in natural masonry materials.

There is a use of cast stone and concrete, partially blackened, which resembles the mortar mixed with soot that is used to point the old naval yard brickwork.

The cast stone is offset with courses of brick; the brick being a deep rose-red. Tiles of soft pink color are also used throughout the walls and facings.

Plaster rendering, in an off-white and light grey, the same

---

6 One of the first iron-clad ships, also preserved in the Portsmouth Dockyard.
7 The portrait, painted in 1515, and reproduced in Margaret Rule, THE MARY ROSE, London 1982, page 14.

color as other brick buildings of the Dockyard. Exterior painted woodwork is used for colonnade details, windows, and doors.

Paving is low-budget asphalt, offset with stone paving in ribbons and bands. Roof tiles are heavy grey slate.

Occasional details, bas-reliefs and incisions, are visible in the concrete and brickwork. These reliefs and incisions add to the feeling of detailed work. They are inexpensively produced with concrete casting techniques—and are colored off-white, black, and rose.

INTERIOR MATERIALS

The intricate main trusses which form the interior of the ship hall are made of smoothly surfaced reinforced concrete similar in texture to cast stone.

The trusses are lace-like, with arches and Tudor roses cut into the concrete, all working structurally together. Although these trusses are of the highest modern technology, in feeling they reach back to works of sixteenth-century architecture like the Henry VII chapel in Westminster Abbey.

Inside, the visitor walks on the stonework of the dry dock; so the paving at the dock level is nineteenth-century ashlar.

The interior of the pageant area is painted woodwork, mainly red and gold, and there are accents of light yellow and black.

VIEWS FROM AROUND THE DOCKYARD

The building volumes form a simple hierarchy of masses which is consistent with the important views from different vantage points throughout the Dockyard.

In particular, there are three very important views: one as you first come around the bow of the *Victory*; another from the drawbridge which forms the entrance to #1 Basin; and another from Brunel's block-making building to the north of the Museum. We have calculated these views, on site, in such a fashion that the new building and its exterior form a harmonious whole with the historic Dockyard forms.

This was the vision of the building as we first conceived it in February 1991. During the next few months we worked carefully with Margaret Rule to refine this vision. After that work the final sequence for the visitor passing through the Museum became slightly different. But in essence—from the point of view of the *feeling* felt by visitors—it is still the same.

CHAPTER TWO

EARLY MODELS AND SKETCHES

Early wood model of the basic building volume: 1:500

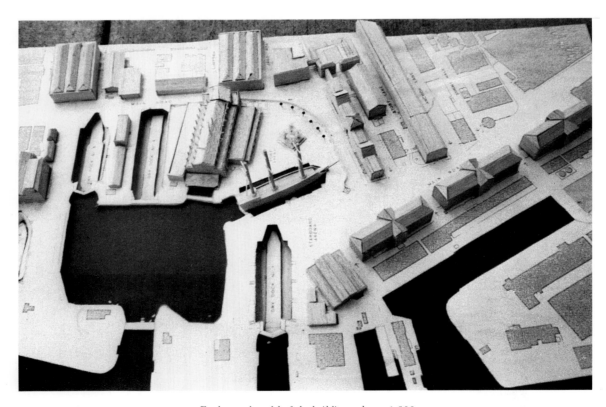

Early wood model of the building volume: 1:500

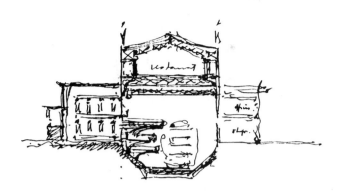

The restaurant above the ship: basic idea

Flags, colonnades, simple structural bays: very early idea

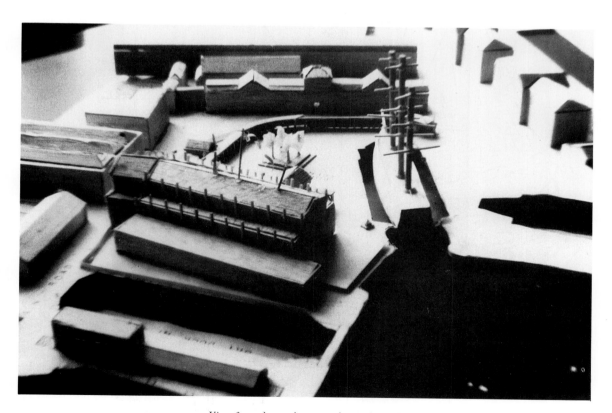

View from the northwest: early wood model

First sketch showing position of the Museum main entrance, in relation to HMS Victory and Victory Arena

A more distant view showing the same thing, with HMS Victory in the foreground

Early notebook sketch of possible structural feeling

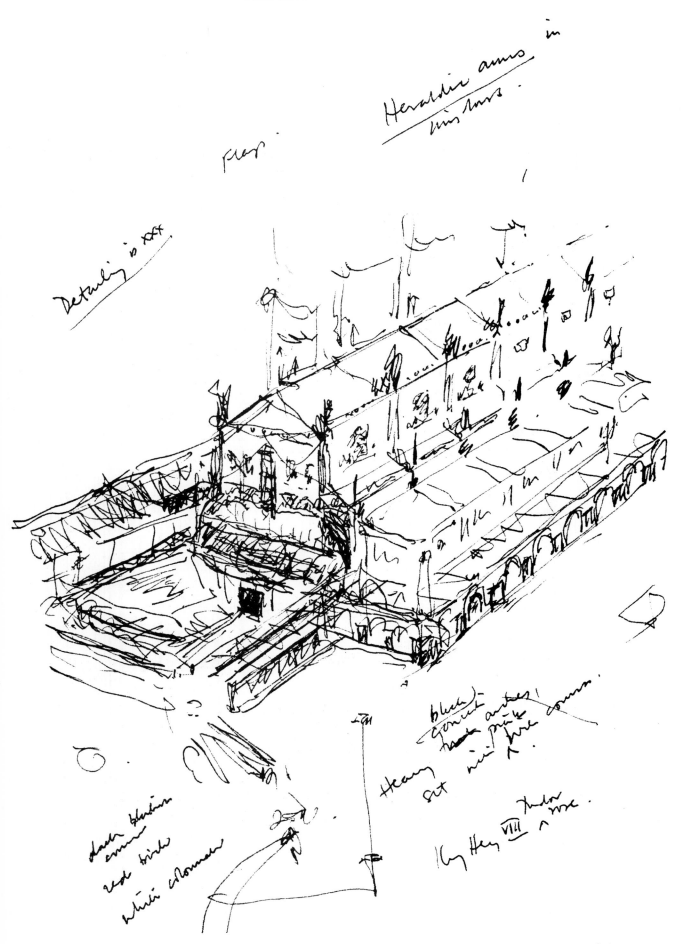

Another very early sketch. Many people found this version too "ecclesiastical." However, it did play an important role in clarifying the nature of the building. Even the "church-like" feeling, though quickly abandoned, helped to establish and intensify the emotional character of the building.

Early paper model of the "ecclesiastical" version

Another view. I brought this model in a big box to show the Prince of Wales. He also found it too church-like, and suggested that we go and look at the medieval abbey barn at Great Coxwell: a building I had read about but had never visited. It was an inspiring and wonderful building, which helped us greatly to transform the ecclesiastical version of spiritual purity, into something more practical and plain and down to earth. A photo of the Great Coxwell Barn can be seen in the background pinned to the wall of the studio.

The very first paper model of the interior and the lace-like concrete trusses. In this model we really had no more than the roughest idea of what these lacy trusses might be like; the model shows a confusion of X-bracing and arches. Even so, the crudeness of this model gave us something to aspire to, and was the precursor of the structural tracery shown on the following pages.

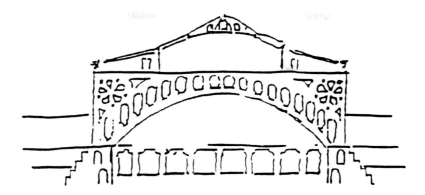

An early sketch showing the lace-like quality of arches and upper truss work. This version, in which the interior trusses would have been visible right up to the floor of the restaurant, later gave way to a version in which the upper plane of the arch became the ceiling.

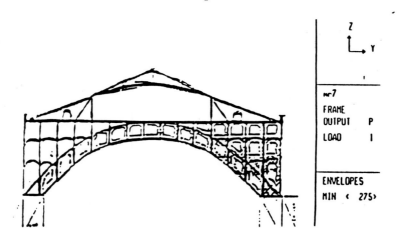

One of the earliest of about seventy computer studies, in which we examined the behavior of different arrangements of ribs, arch tracery, and upper truss combinations

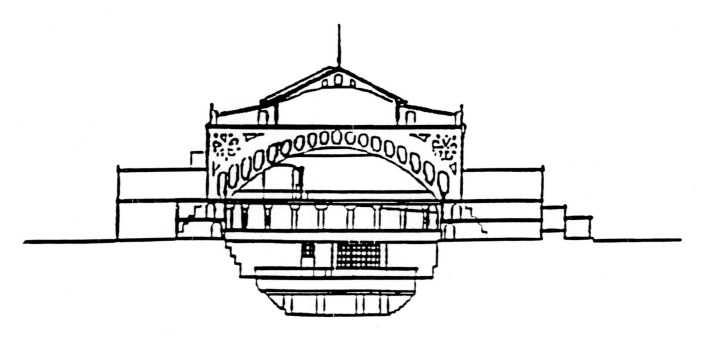

Early interior showing the arch form and gallery to the east

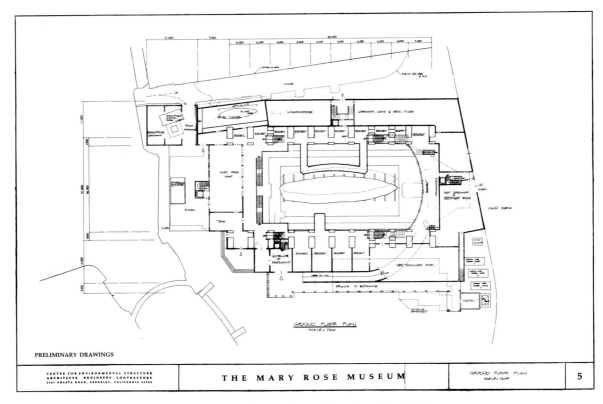

First formal drawings: Ground floor plan, March 1991

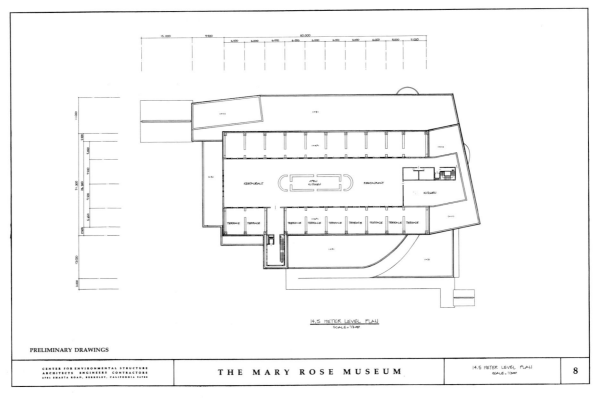

First formal drawings: The restaurant level, March 1991

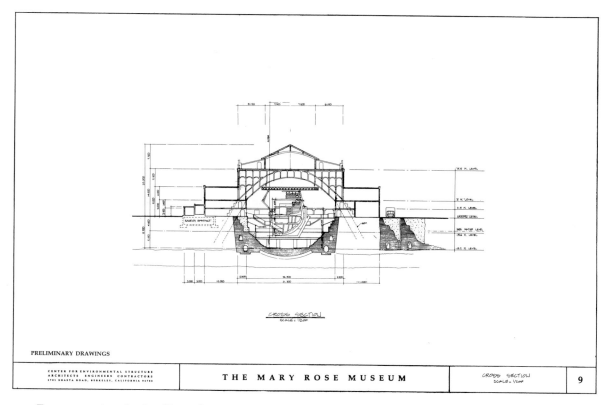

Transverse section, showing ship, arch, restaurant, and galleries, and showing, for the first time, a hint of the foundation problem. March 1991.

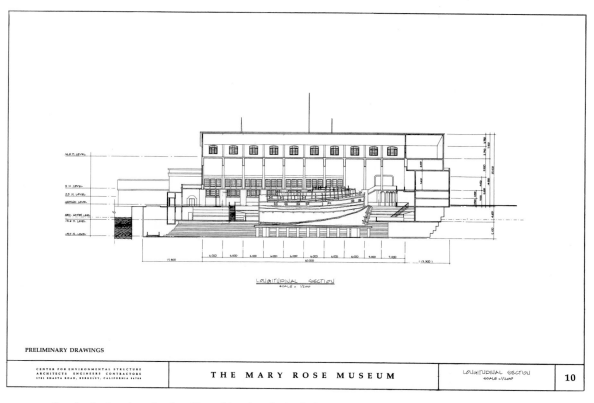

Longitudinal section, showing ship and interior glazing looking from the galleries onto the ship. March 1991.

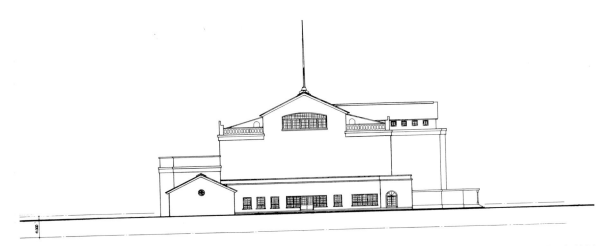

Western elevation, March 1991, showing high peak of the entrance building, leading directly to the roof restaurant. March 1991.

Early sketch, showing the brooding mass of the building, and the feeling — if not the detail — of the construction.

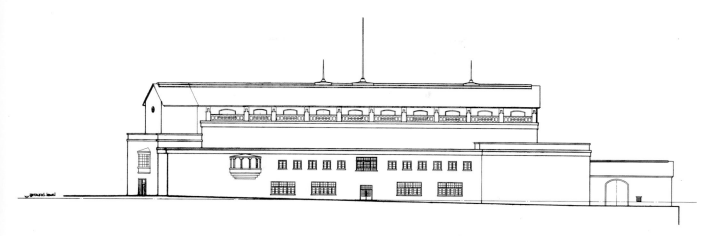

First formal drawing of the north elevation, where Mary Rose Trust offices and laboratories are. Restaurant and terraces visible above.

Another early sketch, showing rooftop terraces served by the restaurant, arched colonnade, and early feeling of ornament

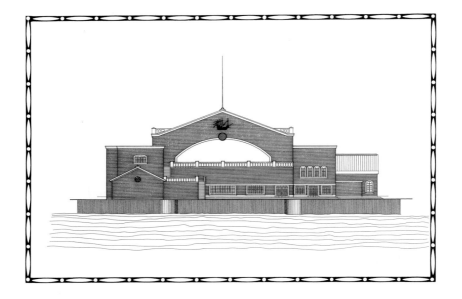

CHAPTER THREE

THE FIRST DESIGN: REALIZING THE VISION

TO REALIZE THIS VISION A NUMBER OF EXTREMELY DIFFICULT TECHNICAL PROBLEMS HAD TO BE SOLVED

The interior of the ship hall is womb-like in cross section, with the exact curve calculated to best display the ship and to transfer the enormous thrusts and forces from the floor and roof above. The space is formed by a series of lace-like arches, double ribbed and intricately detailed. As the ship itself was in the sixteenth century, the arches are a product of the best technology the late twentieth century can afford — but in a profound way they are also ancient. The pageantry, the form, and the details of the structure are all composed precisely to enhance the visitor's appreciation of the life and times of the *Mary Rose*.

The technical brief for realizing the vision we set for ourselves reads like a "mission impossible." It goes something like this: design a structure to span 36 meters, carry the colossal loads of a masonry restaurant full of people positioned at mid-span, and found the footings in a soil that is composed of 10 meters of muck and is subject to differential water content resulting from tidal changes. In addition, make the span out of a material that won't burn in a fire, that won't corrode under the adverse conditions of the preservation regime, and that will last for hundreds of years. To keep as much open space as possible in the adjacent galleries, keep the contact between the superstructure and the ground minimal. And finally, do not make a structure that is a child of the brute-force functional industrial gloom.

No! It has to be as delicate as a butterfly's wing.

GENERAL PHILOSOPHY OF STRUCTURE

Our first thought was to buttress the structural span through a system of buttresses that would be exposed on the outside, much like Herland's 1395 design for spanning the great hall at Westminster.[8] As the analysis proceeded and we began to understand the critical soils conditions that exist at the site and the unusual degree of interaction that would be required between the superstructure and the foundation, it gradually became clear that such a solution would not be possible. And so began the months of design refinement that, when completed, would push modern engineering materials to their limits, would result in over seventy different computer runs of the superstructure alone, and would profoundly tax the ingenuity of our colleagues in foundation engineering.

Our earliest designs showed a roughly semicircular arch resting on large concrete "but-

---

8 Hugh Herland, 1320–1405, master carpenter for King Richard II. Westminster Hall is one of the largest wooden structures of the Gothic period.

Our working model at an early stage of experimentation, showing several competing types of arches juxtaposed

A view of models showing ship, dock, and various arches and trusses

tressed" piers. Some were composed of single arches, but most incorporated a double arch. We tested different patterns of bracing for the double arch, for their visual harmony with the ship, and for structural performance. As the designs unfolded, becoming more concrete, finite element analysis was used to test the schemes structur-ally. This analysis began to re-veal several problems with the designs—including uneven dis-tribution of thrust in the arches, and the negative effect of hori-zontal deflections on the struc-ture. In addition the "feet" were too intrusive in the gallery spaces, the soils analysis was be-ginning to show that the idea of bringing the forces down at a single point might not work, and an unusual degree of harm-ful interplay between the super-structure and foundation was becoming evident.

To begin solving these prob-lems and improve the behavior of the arch, we adjusted the profile of the curve to the exact funicular for the loading of the roof deck and restaurant. Although the

One early arch type, showing X-bracing in center bays, and vertical panels in outer sections.

The #3 dock, showing early version of the full arched truss in its relation to the dock. To grasp the scale it is helpful to remember that the dock is 26 meters wide, and that the lower arch is 13 meters above ground level.

A full view of the model of the dock without the ship. 1:40 scale.

Two neighboring arches, with the X-bracing in the ceiling plane clearly visible

structural behavior improved sharply, even this change could not completely capture the subtle behavior needed.

THE DIAMOND IN ITS SETTING

The central issue, in the whole Museum, is the beauty of the ship. From the outset we thought of the sequence of travel through the Museum, with the most careful thought given to the first glimpses of the ship from the entering ramp, to the first full view seen from the second floor balcony looking down on the ship, to the various views from gallery level, and then the impressive wonderful view looking up at the ship from below — the view from the stone walkway inside the dock at 4.6 meters below the ground.

In all these cases the essential problem of the building is to create the setting for the "diamond." We are intuitively familiar with the idea that a diamond needs a setting, to show it off. The stone, by itself, may be very little to look at. It is the gold filigree, around the stone,

that makes a beautiful diamond ring. The problem of the ship hall is rather similar. Although the ship is beautiful and fascinating, the ship hall must have a physical character which is specifically chosen to set off the

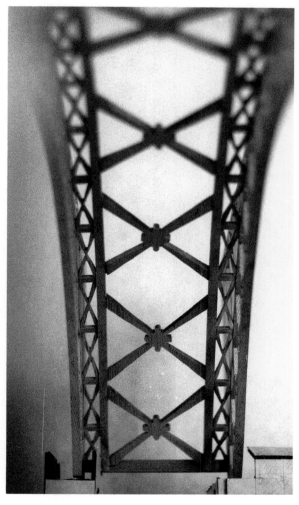

One bay of X-bracing in the ceiling plane. The scale is made beautiful by the small ribbons of X-bracing along the sides, flanking the giant X-braces in the middle.

ship, to intensify its beauty, to focus attention on it.

In our early experiments we had already come to the conclu-

sion that this would be best achieved by a curved vaulted ceiling. We built a very detailed wooden model of the dock at 1:40 scale, with the *Mary Rose* itself also in the model. Then we made various kinds of roof, ceiling, and structural arrangements, very rough ones, studying only the impact on the ship. We asked ourselves, which curve was most beautiful for the ship, and which set the ship off to the most intense degree?

We were able, from our experiments, to determine not only that it needed to be curved, but the character of the curve, its height above the ship, and the way the curve comes down to meet the dock. In short, these experiments told us clearly the precise envelope of the structure, and the precise shape of the interior volume of the ship hall.

It remained only to define the character of the structure itself, which would most beautifully set off the ship, when made to follow the profile of this curving volume.

The result of our work showed us a light and delicate structure, fine in detail, not unlike an enormous version of a

The diamond in its setting. Interior of the ship hall, looking towards the balcony.

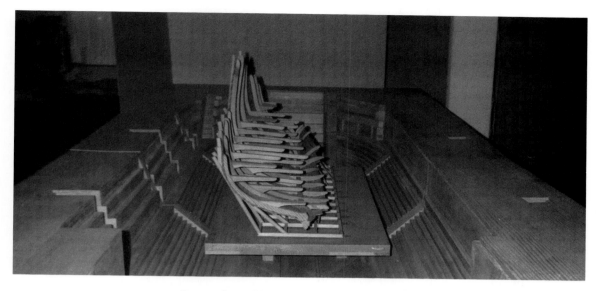

Our wooden model of the ship in the dock. 1:40 scale.

golden filigree around a diamond.

In the second design, described on pages 101–122, we also studied a later, more modest, version where the arches carry less load, and where the arches have a different, simpler kind of structural detailing.

Both are possible. To decide which is really best, further experiments would have to be undertaken. But in any case, the setting of the ship then became the central and most important feature of the Museum.

THE HEIGHT OF THE BUILDING

From the very beginning careful study of the *Victory* site had made it clear to us that what was needed on this site, from the point of view of human feeling, was a massive building, rising up, grey roof, massive walls, a slightly looming presence.

We had been able to make fairly accurate experiments to determine the height of the building—by checking, both from Victory Arena itself, and from the west across the water of #1 Basin. In both instances, the ideal ridge height had been established as upwards of 19 meters.

The feeling of the roof, the shape of the building volume, were not arbitrarily arrived at. It had been established that this building volume was needed—from the point of view of feeling—to support HMS *Victory*. This volume was needed to establish the feeling which is needed to make the Victory Arena and the Mary Rose Museum together function as a punctuation point in the Dockyard, and to create there the feeling of awe and reverence which is appropriate for these two great ships.

It was this background of

experiment which also led to the idea of putting a restaurant on the roof—to keep the volume high. And it was the certainty of this restaurant-on-top idea which then led to the intricate structure for the Museum which is now described—because it was this structure that was required to support the restaurant's rather massive weight.

Note on over-technical thinking about the height, which we rejected.[9] It would have been possible to solve the structure problem by reducing height, or weight. Superficially, this would have had merit, and we would then have gone towards a hangar-type solution. Early in the project some engineers we consulted urged vehemently that this should be done. But such a solution would have missed the point. What is needed for this site is a volume of just this shape, height, and proportion. This is what is needed to heal, and make great, this particular bit of earth in Portsmouth Dockyard. To

9 This and the following notes on over-technical thinking are intended to show, by contrast, how a certain type of highly exaggerated technical thinking—though today often considered normal and appropriate—in fact goes far to excess, and removes the balance between technique and feeling which is necessary in a building.

Volume of the first design seen from the southeast, with HMS Victory *in the background. The masts of* Mary Rose *as they penetrate the roof of the Museum, show the actual positions and heights of masts, in relation to the ship hull in the dock.*

The same model, from the western end, HMS Victory *on the right, and the café terrace visible just behind the balustrade that forms the water's edge of #1 Basin.*

back away from it, just because it is hard to solve technically, would have betrayed the beauty of the Dockyard, for the sake of a cheap, quick fix.

The real solution lies in the fact that the final structure has the height, has the weight, has the volume, and still manages to solve the technical problems at the right price, while keeping the feeling intact.

SOLVING THE FOUNDATION PROBLEM

From the first moment of our contact with the Mary Rose Trust, and especially after understanding the great arch structure that is needed to provide the diamond with its setting, we knew that the foundation design would be the key to the design of the Museum, and that soil testing and sampling must begin immediately, to give us a clear understanding of what lay beneath the surface.

Our analysis of the building design had concluded that the setting of the "diamond" required that the interior of the ship hall must have arches which would span the dock, and which would also create a proper setting for the ship. Because of the building's height restriction (imposed by surroundings), and volume restriction (imposed by heating and ventilating and mechanical air-system considerations), it was necessary that these arches be somewhat shallow. Yet the shallower the arch, the greater the horizontal thrusts. It was inevitable that the building would create massive horizontal thrusts. How should these thrusts be contained?

Aerial view of the same model, from the south. This view shows the trellised wall, and arched arbors which provided seating along the curved perimeter of Victory Arena. This is an early version of the model in which the main volume of the ship hall included a bent portion at the extreme eastern end that was later removed in response to the Planning Officer's request for a less massive volume.

Pen and ink study of the main entrance and main colonnade

The foundations of the building would lie in fill next to the dry dock, material which was fill from the time of the dock's original construction, that might include random rubble, rotted wood, mud, remnants of old structures, and other debris of the last three centuries. It could not be counted on to provide much support. However, the horizontal thrusts which would be produced by the arches of the building had to be resisted and contained below ground. In addition, the thrust lines would intersect an adjacent dry dock exerting unacceptable pressure there.

In our cost picture for the building shell we had determined that the sum of £548,000 ($932,000) and no more, could be spent on the foundation (not including slabs).

It is important to digress here to matters which will be covered in more detail later. In the form of design and construction management we have pioneered, the broad cost picture for a building is part of the design process from the beginning. We had a budget of £5 million (some $8.5 million) for the building shell, within about £10 million for the building as a whole, and results of our initial cost allocation for making the best building for the available budget left just £548,000 for the foundation. To maintain the balance of the carefully thought-out vision of the building, we knew this balanced cost picture had to be kept, from the beginning. If, for example, because of technical difficulty the cost of the foundation were to go to £800,000 or £900,000 ($1.36 million or $1.53 million), this would then remove some other essential feature of the building—and as a balanced and beautiful thing, the building would then lose its quality even from the very beginning.

It is important to realize that when the first reports came in on the actual soil conditions, our colleagues at PSA-BMSE (see footnote on page 98) did in fact tell us that the foundation they recommended would cost £850,000 plus. We firmly rejected their recommended £850,000 foundation, and went to work to design a cheaper foundation capable of supporting the building loads under the

The final model of the first design, scale 1:200, seen from the south

difficult subsoil conditions. We did finally succeed in designing a foundation for £548,000.

We solved the problem by employing a modified form of the technique which had been proposed to us by our colleagues at PSA-BMSE. They had suggested a deep wall, 20 meters deep and one meter thick, which would run the length of the building at the main supports. The depth of the wall would act like a pile, taking vertical loads well below the dock, thus eliminating surcharge on the masonry dock structure. At the same time the huge surface area of the wall would act through bending and passive resistance of the soil, and would be capable of providing the horizontal resistance to counter the huge thrust of the

arches—about 300,000 lbs—on each column base.

This deep wall would be dug by special equipment essentially like a bucket drag-line, with liquid clay (bentonite) pumped in continuously to prevent cave-in from the surrounding soil. The difficulty was that the technique, when costed out, still came in at about £800,000, which is about £250,000 over our cost allocation.

We went to work to modify the PSA proposal with the goal of drastically reducing cost. We finally developed a T-shaped barrette—which also had a 20-meter depth and which could be excavated by the same equipment—but which had a far lower volume, thus reducing excavation and concrete costs, but

which, because of the stiffness provided by the upright of the T and the passive resistance still provided by the bar of the T, would provide the same effective horizontal resistance accomplished by the more expensive proposal. This technique was an invention—apparently unknown among foundation contractors who have developed the deep wall foundation—and further analysis to refine the details remains to be done. But we had succeeded in bringing the foundation costs to £548,000 set in our cost allocation. A workable solution to the foundation design had been found, and the "cost problem" had been solved.

Note on over-technical thinking about the foundation, which we rejected. It would have been possible to solve the foundation problem in an entirely different fashion: by redefining the building as a hangar with 45-meter trusses forming a flat roof, and spanning from side to side. This box solution would have imposed little or no horizontal thrust on the foundation structure, and

would therefore have been technically "easy." But we had already determined that the spirit of the Museum required a setting for the ship; and, in early studies, that the site required a relatively high building mass. If we had given in to the positivistic and "obvious" technical solution, the environment would

have been irrevocably damaged, at a loss to the human spirit.

The over-technical solution only seems to work if you pretend that the human spirit and human feeling are not real. The real trick is to find a superb bit of technical invention which is consistent with the human spirit.

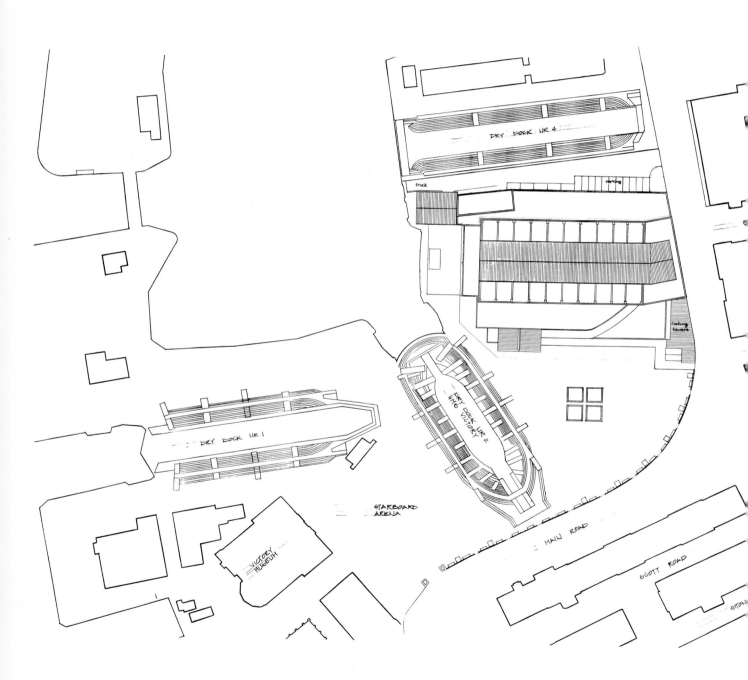

Site plan, showing HMS Victory *nearby dry dock #4 and Mary Rose Museum*

BUILDING PLANS AT SIX LEVELS

The drawings on the next pages show the plans of the building at 9.7 meters below ground (the floor of the dock), 4.6 meters below ground (the stone walkway level, halfway down inside the dock), ground level (USA first floor), first floor level (USA second floor), second floor level (USA third floor), and at the restaurant level high on the roof of the Museum.

PLAN AT 9.7 METERS BELOW GROUND LEVEL. This plan shows the laboratory working areas beneath the ship's cradle. The small square elements are the brick piers which carry the steel barge. The ship itself lies on that barge.

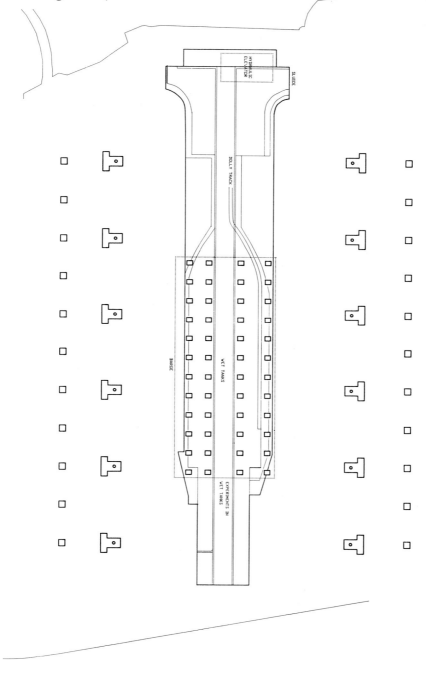

Plan at 9.7 meters below ground level

On this plan the barge is shown raised, as directed by Margaret Rule, to improve viewing of the ship, and to create effective headroom in the area below the barge so that conservation work can continue there.

Outside the ship hall, at the western end of the dock, there is a large working area served by a hydraulic elevator.

The drawing also shows the T-barrettes which act as foundations for the ship hall's massive piers.

PLAN AT 4.6 METERS BELOW GROUND LEVEL. This

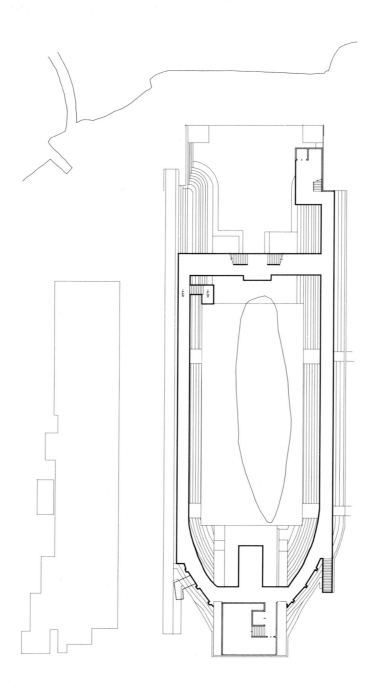

Plan at 4.6 meters below ground level

is the best viewing level for the ship. The plan shows a concrete walkway which goes around the inside of the dock. This walkway is an extension of the existing stone walkway that is part of the historic dock itself. Access to this level is from stairs at the west end, near the museum shop and from existing stairs at the east end. The plan shows the location of stairs and elevators.

GROUND FLOOR PLAN (USA FIRST FLOOR). Here we see the main entrance, auditorium, ground floor galleries on the south side, where guns and exhibits will be placed, and a

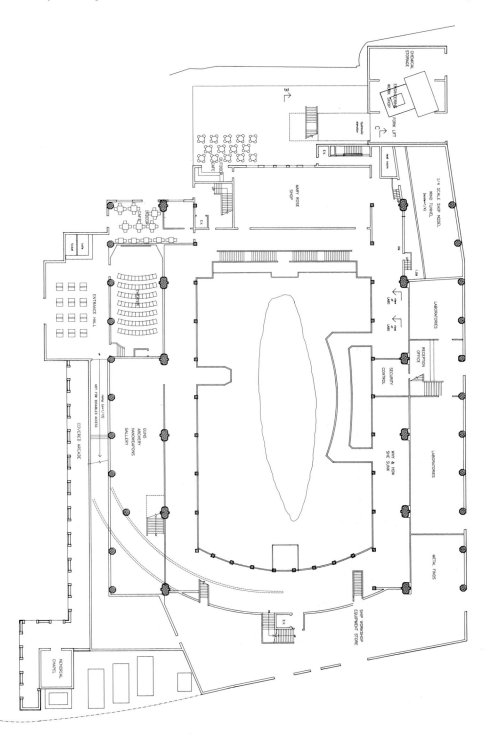

Ground floor plan (USA first floor)

ground floor gallery for scientific exhibits on the north side. The north side also includes offices for the Mary Rose Trust and conservation laboratories. The museum shop appears at the west end of the ship hall. On the way out visitors pass the large working ship model of the *Mary Rose* in a special room built to the northwest corner of the ship hall.

FIRST FLOOR PLAN (USA SECOND FLOOR). Here we see the first floor galleries on the south side including social exhibits, exhibits showing the life of the men, food and drink,

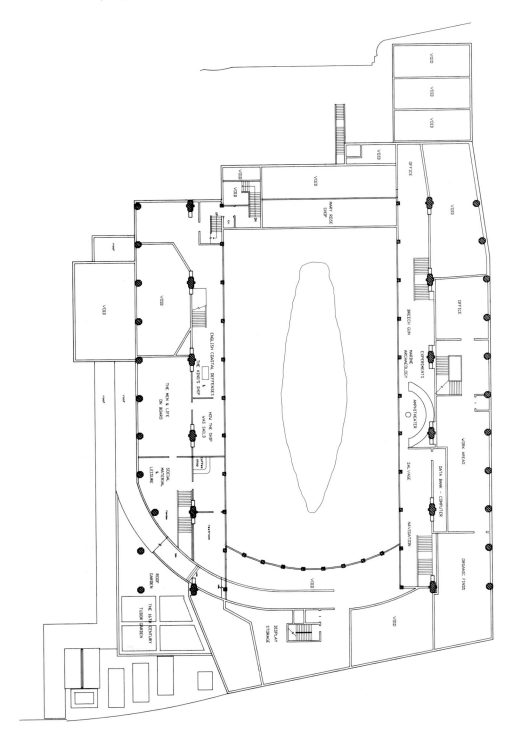

First floor plan (USA second floor)

weapons, ship-building, and so on.

The north side includes further scientific exhibits, with a small miniature auditorium for demonstrations. The grand balcony at the rear of the ship hall is also visible at this level.

SECOND FLOOR PLAN (USA THIRD FLOOR). Visitors approach the ship from the second floor, after going up the entrance ramp. The ramp brings visitors to the bay window on the north side of the building, looking down to dock #4.

The high level gallery also gives a beautiful bird's-eye view

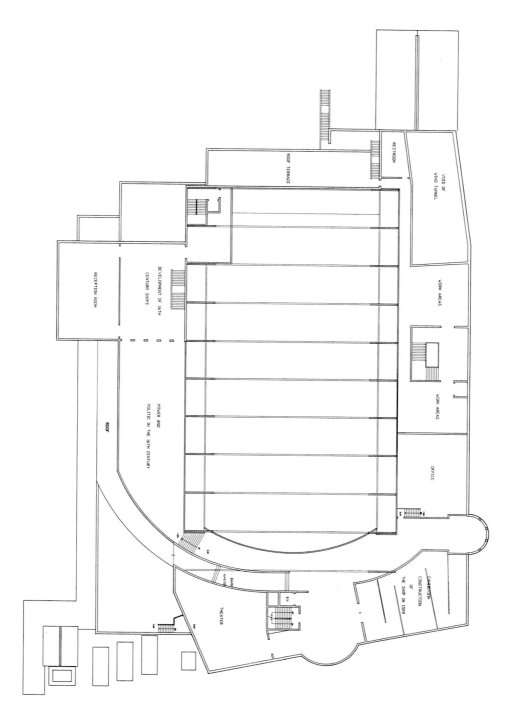

Second floor plan (USA third floor)

of the *Mary Rose* itself, for the first time. The second floor gallery on the south side contains the first main exhibit: the field-of-the-cloth-of-gold showing the panoply of Henry VIII's reign. The north side of the building includes offices, conservation laboratories and workshops.

PLAN AT 14 METERS ABOVE GROUND: RESTAURANT LEVEL. The restaurant, high above the Dockyard, commands a beautiful view of the surrounding docks and waterways. Access to the restaurant is by elevator, from inside and outside the Museum. To the south there are sheltered sunny terraces, for lunch and evening meals, overlooking HMS *Victory*.

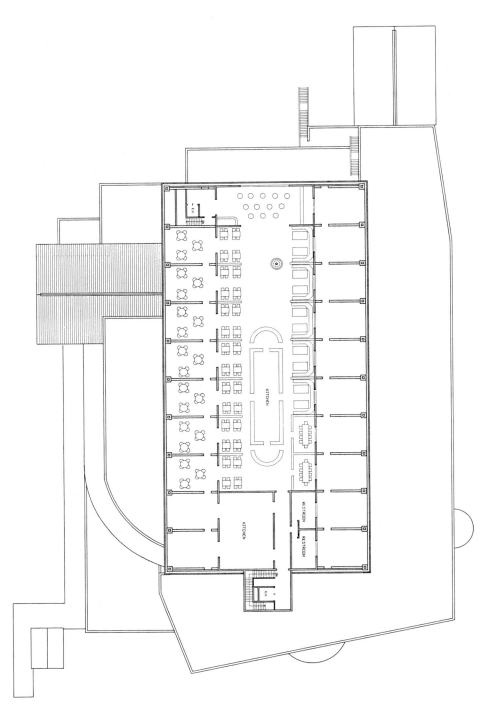

Plan at 14 meters above ground level (restaurant level)

CONCRETE LATTICE ARCHES

From the beginning it had seemed that arches would be needed for the great span of the ship hall, in order to create elements of a fitting size which would complement the ship.

The ship, in cross section, is roughly elliptical. The dock is constructed from a series of stone steps which when taken together form a roughly inverted arch. To complete the space, that is to make the space formed by the dock whole, and to form a setting for the ship, the upper part of the hall needs to be curved to match the dock. The exact sweep of the curve, the precise tightness or closeness to the ship, and the details of the structure must be carefully orchestrated to respect both the ship and the space.

To achieve these goals the arch needs to spring from the innermost edge of the dock, forming in space a rough mirror image of the dock stonework. The tip of the ship's oval needs to reach upwards to the central apex of the arch, and be almost touching it. And the dimension of the arches has to be substantial. Achieving the delicate balance of these requirements is crucial. Make the arch too high and the ship feels lost in the belly of a cavern that is too big to display it correctly. Make the arch too wide, by springing it from a point further away from the dock edge, and the ship gets lost in the space and the beautiful shape and curve of the dock are destroyed. Make the arches too skinny and they won't have enough dimension to set up a rhythm of repeating arches necessary to form the curving

space. After studying models, it seemed to us that these arches needed to have a considerable depth to make the hall feel right.

Beyond the impact of these spatial and geometrical issues, the arch shape is appropriate as a structure. It is an efficient form capable of resisting both vertical and lateral loads in compression. Given the height of the building, its proximity to the water and potential susceptibility to wind damage, and the weight of a rather large restaurant above it, positioned at mid-span, an arched compression system is a good choice theoretically and one which would tend to keep costs down.

Making such a structure work in this particular case, however, proved to be an extremely difficult task, requiring thousands of hours of computer studies to examine the detailed behavior of the superstructure on its own, and in combination with its interaction with the foundation and the soil surrounding the dock.

From the very first structural sketches we had already been led to an arch depth of about 2.4 meters. With the additional possibility that this arch would be punctured by latticework, to reduce weight, and thereby in effect adding strength, and further complementing the "diamond setting," we were led naturally to the idea of a double arch, top and bottom, with the latticework in between.

A true arch, or more correctly a pure compression arch, carries its internal forces as compression with no interior shear or bending. Because of the efficient use of material such an arch tends to be relatively thin in cross section and is

therefore flexible (in the case of a double arch, the flexibility can be assured by an appropriate pattern of connection between the upper and lower arches). One advantage to this flexible form is that when the foundation deflects laterally (moves outward) under the horizontal thrusts (which the soil around the dock will permit) no adverse forces are generated inside the superstructure. The arch changes shape slightly but continues to behave in compression. The disadvantages are twofold. On the one hand this form produces extremely large horizontal forces which must be resisted at the ground, exacerbating an already serious problem with the foundation; and on the other hand any change in loading, such as an asymmetrical live load on the restaurant decks, has to be dealt with by either stiffening the arch or stiffening the deck.

A fully stiffened arch, where the latticework between the upper and lower arches connect the two rigidly, has disadvantages as well. The most serious of these is that lateral displacement of the foundation when the arch spreads, will cause extremely large moments near the base and apex of the structure.

Aside from these concerns, there was also the question of whether or not a double arch could be made to carry its loads in such a way as to bring approximately equal flow of force in the upper and lower arches: something essential for efficient behavior.

We made a number of preliminary models along the lines of a double arch, with various kinds of lattice structure in the middle, forming a truss-like

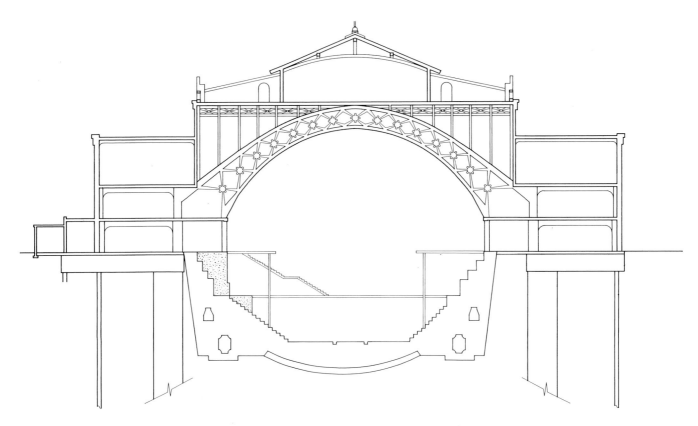

Major cross section, at the massive piers

arch or connected double arch. At the very beginning we hung strings, upside down, in the natural catenary position, with weights hung along them, to see how the double arch system would behave, and to find out if it was even possible to make the forces flow smoothly through the two arches together — or whether one or the other would tend to attract all the forces into itself. Our string models showed that it was possible, in principle, to divide the flow of compression evenly between the two.

In contrast, however, and to complicate matters further, there was the problem that the dock edge and the attendant dock could not be counted on to bear any significant load. This feature of the configuration caused a serious problem. On the one

hand, we were confronted with an architectural situation that required we have the arch hug the edge of the dock — to make the space of the nave beautiful and to display the ship correctly. This view is consistent with an equal force distribution between the two arches. Yet on the other hand we couldn't bring any load down onto the dock edge, instead having to send the loads several meters away from the edge.

During the course of the project we studied over seventy different finite element (computer) models of the structure in which we tried different configurations of load, struts, arches, and supports — each one constructed to address one or more of the problems enumerated above, and to increase our own

understanding of the real behavior and interaction between the superstructure and the foundation. Examples of output from different computer models are shown on pages 68–69.

The computer modelling was vital. Not only did the computer models help us to solve the problem by giving us technical information about stresses and strains, but they also served to educate us about the structural behavior, so that we could make intelligent design decisions with respect to *all* of the problems — architectural, structural, and constructional.

Throughout the course of the studies we looked at various interior lattice arrangements; some which allowed the two arches to behave somewhat independently and others which

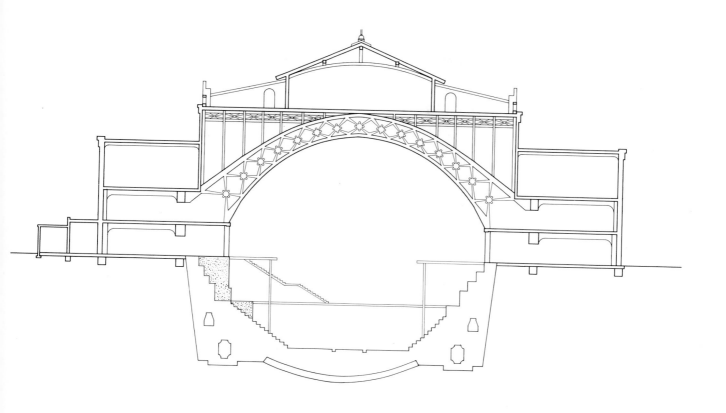

Major cross section, intermediate, between the massive piers

forced them to work together like the top and bottom chords of a truss.

At the conclusion of this series of studies we had invented a structure which might be termed a "selectively stiffened arch." The majority, but not all of the compression forces travelled through the outer, or upper arch, delivering the forces to the beams and columns at the third floor. This solved the problems with the dock edge and also solved out-of-plane buckling problems with the arch because the top chord is more easily braced against such action. The bottom chord then served to "selectively stiffen" the arch so that it could handle different load conditions such as wind and asymmetrical live loads, and also reduce the amount of horizontal thrust produced while simultaneously allowing the much needed flexibility in the overall arch structure—so that lateral movement of the foundation did not create intolerable forces in the superstructure. Although further work is needed to check the structure and finalize and confirm the preliminary findings, it appears that we have solved all of the major contingencies.

THE NATURE OF THE ARCHES

The arch structure which evolved is a balanced structure: the size of the arches, their lace-like character, the particular curve—are all connected. This connectedness doesn't happen by paying attention to any one parameter exclusively. It comes about by considering all parameters together in such a way that each parameter influences and is influenced by each of the others. This process of design is quite different from the normal process in which the so-called "architecture" is concerned only with form and the so-called "engineering" is then concerned with making it work technically.

In the arches, for example, we can identify four principal parameters: the depth of the arch, the spacing of the arches, the structural behavior of the arch, and the exact geometry between the ends of the arch and the supporting structure. Each of these four must work together with the others to create a harmonious structure. A change in

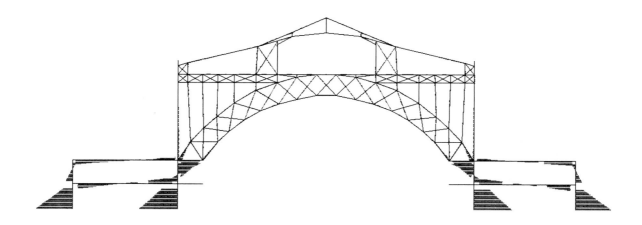

Computer output showing bending moments for version MR70

any one of them will immediately have impact on the other three.

During our seventy computer simulations we kept on focussing on one particular parameter at a time, while paying strict attention to the others. A solution for any one parameter which caused problems for the others was always rejected.

The reason the arches are beautiful is precisely that no single parameter was given preference. All parameters — spacing, depth, structural efficiency, connection to the galleries and supporting structure — were handled in a way that found that solution for each one which simultaneously most benefitted the others.

HEATING AND VENTILATING THE GREAT VOLUME OF THE SHIP HALL

From the outset, we were faced with a considerable challenge, the problem of heating and ventilating. The ship hall is, by its very nature, enormous, and running costs for heating

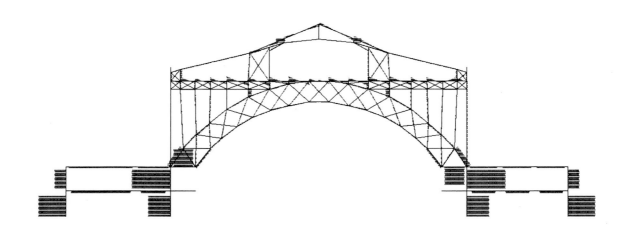

Computer output showing shear forces for version MR70

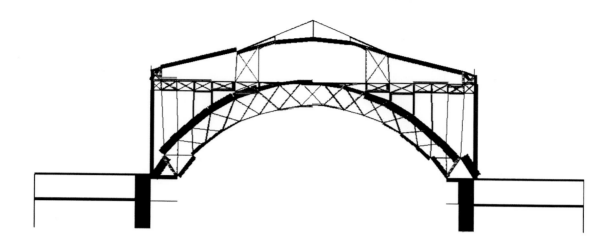

Computer output of axial forces: version MR70

and ventilating are a significant issue. This enormous volume must be carefully conditioned with regard to temperature and humidity. A carefully controlled environment is most essential now, during the conservation phase, but it will remain important after the year 2020, when the *Mary Rose* is stabilized.

To confirm our own intuition that our idea of a cocoon within a cocoon (ship hall surrounded by galleries, and a restaurant with heated space on top) would perform well thermally, we elicited a report from our consulting engineer, David Sidebotham at PSA-BMSE. We specifically asked him to compare the running cost of our building with its large ship hall volume, with the running cost of the somewhat smaller ship hall in the John Winter design that had been rejected by the Prince of Wales,[10] but had at one time been accepted by the Mary Rose Trust from a heating-ventilating point of view. Mr. Sidebotham's analysis follows:

Analysis of Ship Hall
We have made a basic assumption that the area occupied by the viewing public will be the same in both the CES and Winter designs at about 2000 m². There remains therefore a volume increase of 11% associated solely with the ship hall. However, this is a very small percentage increase and will lead to little or no increase in capital cost of plant for the ship hall between the two designs.
Annual heating running costs (very approximate, ship hall only) are also similar; the CES design perhaps costing another £1,000 ($1,700) per year to run.
The above statements ignore the effect of the different mass of the two designs, and the different thermal storage effects that go with them. The higher thermal mass of the CES design will even out temperature variation through the day, and to some extent from day to day. Thermal storage increases the time constant of the building which will reduce the instantaneous demand on the heating system and will enable smaller plant to be installed in the CES design. Thermal mass also stores excess energy, which would otherwise have to be removed from the building, thus maintaining temperatures later in the day when heating would otherwise be needed. The CES design has distinct advantages and will result in energy saving over the lighter Winter design.
The above analysis assumes a simple air change rate regime. If the ship hall is air-conditioned both capital and running costs will be increased, though the differential between the CES and Winter designs will be imperceptible.
The larger thermal storage of the CES design will also greatly reduce the cooling demand in summer and will result in smaller plant sizes and lower running costs than the Winter design.
It will also be possible to incorporate energy saving measures on both designs including recovery of heat from exhaust air streams, and the use of water from the adjacent basin both as a heat source for heating and a heat sink for cooling. The temperature in the basin is also frequently low enough for it to be used directly for free cooling. All of which has distinct advantages for energy conservation.

10 See discussion on page 12.

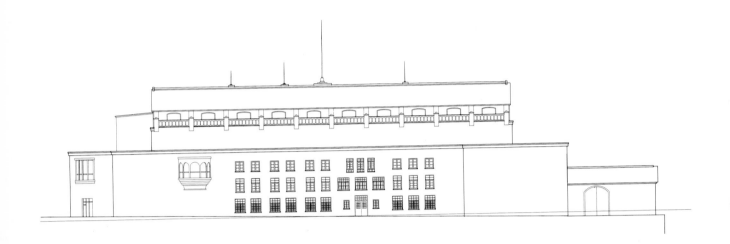

North elevation, from dock #4

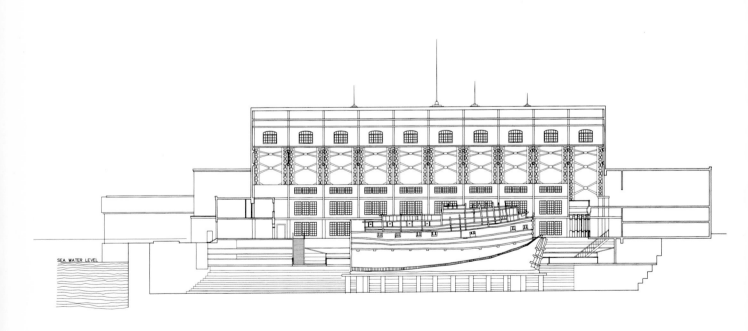

SEA WATER LEVEL

Interior longitudinal section

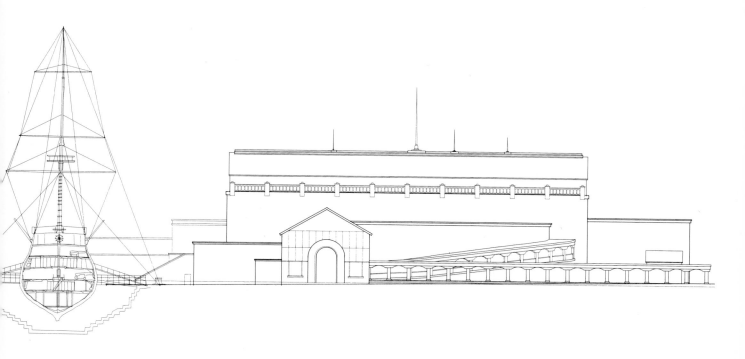

South elevation, from Victory Arena

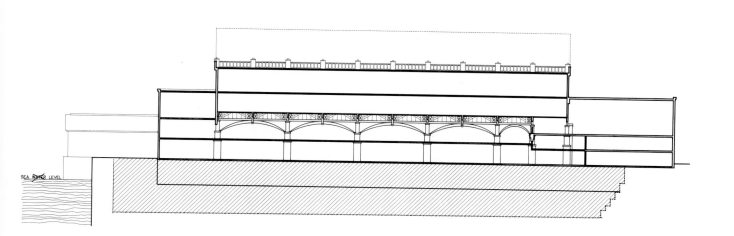

Longitudinal section showing secondary support arches

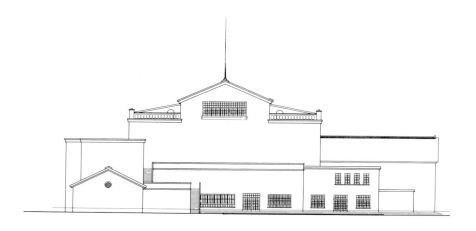

West elevation: the view from the water

THE CLEANING PROBLEM

The atmosphere of the ship hall interior, during the conservation years from 1994 to 2020, will be moist and warm, a condition which will support the growth of algae and molds on the interior surfaces. During the first twenty-five years cleaning the ship hall will therefore be of great importance.

The accompanying drawing shows the travelling gantry crane, suspended from the ship hall arches, and shows the way in which it provides continuous access to the arches and ceiling for steam cleaning.

The structure itself is designed to be made of a dense, compact concrete with a non-porous, very smooth, surface which is easy to clean.

In order to provide access to the underside of the ceiling, and to the lacework of the arches, the gantry crane is designed to follow the arch. It is a curved girder, with a stepped cleaning platform. This brings each point on the underside of the ceiling,

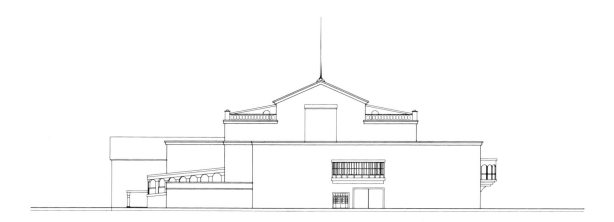

East elevation: view from Dockyard road

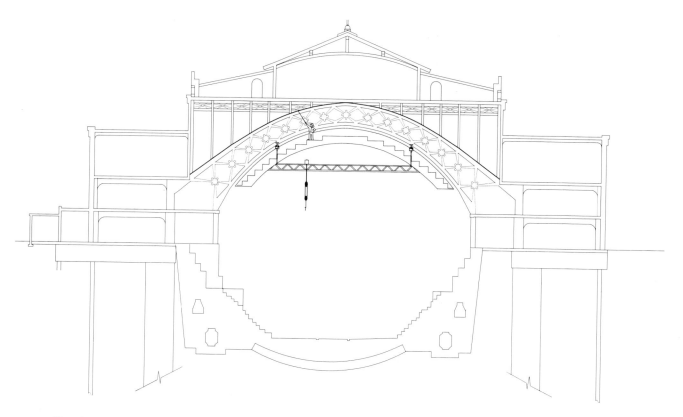

The solution of the cleaning problem. The travelling gantry crane, built for access to ship during conservation operations, runs on rails hung from the arches. It is equipped with a bridged platform close to the ship hall arches for cleaning operations. As required by brief, every part of the lacework arches, is accessible to a man with a five-foot steam-cleaning wand. When not in use, the travelling gantry is run to the far end of the ship hall, and is virtually invisible.

and every point of the arches themselves, within reach of a worker on the gantry equipped with a five-foot steam cleaning wand.

DOUBLING THE DISTANCE BETWEEN SUPPORTS

During 1991 a controversy about column spacing arose in our work with Museum directors. The discussion of this matter ultimately benefitted the museum design greatly.

We had envisaged the Museum, from the beginning, as a structure which was supported on a large number of columns, with vaults among these col-

umns. These elements would create beautiful bays and spaces where the museum exhibits would be at home.

Some Museum directors, with a background in the construction of commercial space, believed that, on the contrary, the museum space should be neutral space, uninterrupted continuous space, on the model of a department store or supermarket, which could then be subdivided in any way according to the wishes of future Museum administrators. This was the famous "flexible space" beloved by architects and commercial planners during the mid-twentieth century.

The following brief excerpt

from a memorandum to the Mary Rose Trust chief executive John Vimpany, gives the flavor of the discussion in its early stages:

I would like to add a general comment about the issue of flexibility. Margaret relayed to me, your feeling that the museum space should be flexible, for the benefit of future exhibits, future museum directors, and so on, and told me that this concern had been expressed by Martyn (Vesey) and by yourself from the perspective of exhibition design. Of course I am well aware that the conventional wisdom about modern architecture has in recent decades shown a preference for this so-called "flexible" space. This is familiar from office buildings, super markets, department stores, and occasionally too, from some museums. However, you should know that this conventional wisdom about a type of

Old version: Six-meter structural bays: each truss comes down onto a column

New version: Twelve-meter structural bays: alternating trusses are supported on a longitudinal arch

building are more profoundly integrated. In many cases it turns out that space which contains columns, is more usable, not less usable: and that the stereotype of flexible uninterrupted space is to some degree in error.

We were not able to win this argument. Although, in fact, we felt the museum space would be more beautiful if spaces were smaller, and clearly articulated by columns, our instructions were to make the bays larger, to allow for "flexibility" in laying out exhibits. The observable fact that columned space such as that provided in the Dockyard's 1798 Paymaster Building, or in Boathouse #6, is more flexible, not less—because it creates naturally articulated spaces, and comfortable half open boundaries between spaces—was overwhelmed by this concern about the notion of flexibility.

In view of the very strong feelings expressed to us by the Trust, we accepted the revised brief, given to us in December 1991, and met a new set of conditions in which the column bays were to be bigger, and in which at least one gallery space was to have a clear open space of 6×18 meters. Later, in February 1992, we were asked to place the columns even *further* apart. The open spaces in the museum gallery areas were to be made even larger than before. This introduced great difficulty for the structure.

The great weight of the structure, already difficult to handle, now had to come down on supports still further apart. To solve this problem, we finally decided to introduce a second system of arches, running the length of the ship hall, so that literally half of the supports could be removed, and half the downward thrust, instead of coming down to the

neutral uninterrupted space which is considered "flexible" is somewhat out of date, and perhaps represents the best of 1950–1970's thinking. The more modern position about this question is now tending to recognize many practical, technical, and emotional problems in- *herent in this "endless space" type of solution. Recent buildings have begun to move away from the 1950–70's thinking, and have begun accepting a more solid, and less flimsy type of structure where exhibition, shop, or office spaces and the load-bearing structure of the* ground, would now come down on the new arches, and would be transferred through them, to the remaining piers and into the foundation.

This seemingly simple idea made it necessary to take materials to their maximum capacity. As we wrote to Margaret Rule:

May 11, 1992
Dear Margaret,
We have succeeded in making a structural design with six major columns on either side. In this design, the column-to-column spacing, longitudinally, is 12 meters on center. This is twice the spacing of the previous design. The ground floor plan works out as shown. The small nibs on either side of the columns are to provide support for a longitudinal arch. Columns on the first floor (drawing not yet done) are also at 12-meter centers in the longitudinal direction.
The arch-trusses spanning the dock remain at 6 meters on center, and every other one of these arches comes down on a major column. It is not structurally practical to increase the spacing of the arches. The intermediate arch-trusses come down on a longitudinal arch. These longitudinal arches are visible in the longitudinal section. We are also sending you two cross sections, one at the major column position, and one at the longitudinal mid-arch position.
This has required enormous computer time, and lengthy and detailed engineering work. Loads are high, and sections and materials are stretched to the limit. We confirmed the feasibility of the superstructure in this method a few days ago . . .

Thus, the problem had been solved. The clear spans needed by the Trust, had been provided without loss of efficiency or beauty of the structure.

Note on over-technical thinking about increasing distance between supports, which we rejected. The technical point of view which comes naturally from

warehouse architecture is that of flexible space. In this purely technical view, one simply builds a gigantic space frame, spans the space from outside to outside, with no interior supports at all. This space is "flexible" in the jargon, and one might use it as office, museum gallery, warehouse.

Of course, such a solution is technically possible. Gigantic spans like those at the Tokyo International Airport are capable of carrying space frames over hundreds of feet.

But the feeling of the space created underneath is negligible. In the case of a museum, above all, the exhibits need space, they need to feel the weight of massive space; the space needs to be defined, emotionally, by structure: the visitor feels the building, and feels the museum exhibits inside the building. There is no virtue whatsoever, from an emotional point of view, in making clear-span space — any more than the cathedral at Salisbury would be improved emotionally if the nave columns were removed to provide clear-span space, or any more than the Parthenon would be improved it if were clear-span space. In these buildings, and in all great buildings, it is the impact of the columns, the load bearing elements, on the space, and the interplay of columns, beams, and space, which ultimately create the emotional weight of the building.

When all is said and done, however, we believe that the dialogue with our clients made the building design better. The way in which the larger arched bays carry the load with a double system of arches, gives the building a mutually arrived-at magnificence which it would otherwise not have had. Thus the argument, though fierce, did end with a collaboration which helped to make the building better.

BUILDING OVER THE EXISTING TENT

The drawings on pages 76–77 show the way in which the Museum is built as a four-step process, with the existing temporary fabric tent staying in place until the end.[11]

One of the things which had been made clear from the beginning was that the ship was very sensitive indeed, to the conservation process—and that the cold-water regime (up to 1994) and the hot-water regime with dissolved chemicals (1994 to 2020) would have to continue uninterrupted while the building was being built, and while visitors visited, through every phase of construction.

We therefore had to find a way of building the Museum in such a fashion that the existing tent could be left in place, throughout construction, and then removed only at the very last minute, after the new hall was conditioned and operational in its controlled environment.

This meant that the span of the new ship hall had to go over the tent, and contain the tent completely. It posed an immense structural challenge. We had determined that the museum galleries and columns, must, from a spatial point of view, come to the edge of the dock. This was necessary, in our judgment, to provide adequate enclosure for the ship. It was necessary, in order to create a beautiful and comfortable edge to the dock. And it was necessary in order to create an emotionally coherent structure.

Unfortunately, however, the existing dock, being stone, is not

---

11 From 1982 until 1993 the tent was fabric over an aluminum frame. At the time of writing, it is possible that this fabric will soon be reinforced with GRP (glass-reinforced plastic) to lengthen its life. Whether this is done or not, the permanent Museum can be built over the tent, reinforced or unreinforced, at any time in its life.

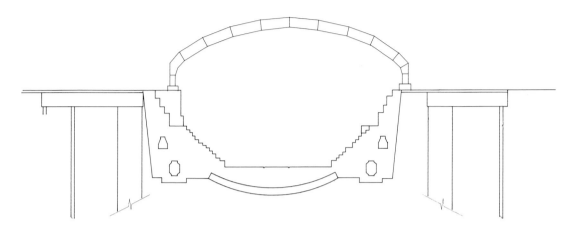

Step 1: The existing tent in place

capable of taking any substantial loads, and this condition is most serious on the south side, where an unstable 19th century concrete fill aggravates the situation. It is therefore necessary that all major loads come down on main supports at least five meters back from the edge of the dock. Placing the supports five meters back from the edge of the dock has one key benefit. It is consistent with the requirement that the new museum structure be built over the existing tent without touching it or penetrating it.

What we did, therefore, was to design the arches in such

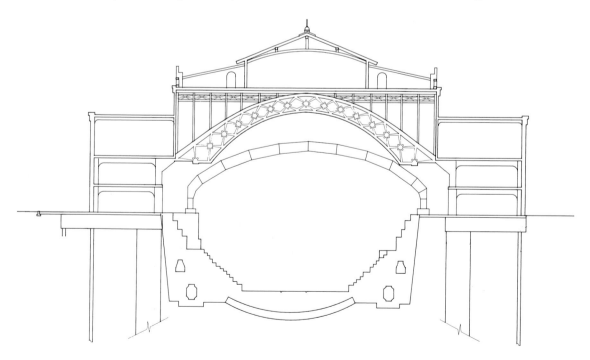

Step 2: The new superstructure built to enclose the tent

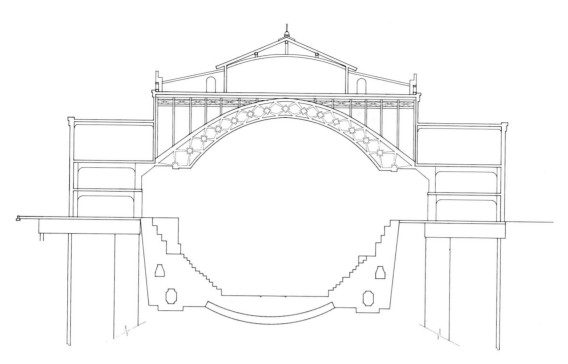

Step 3: Removal of the tent, within the new ship hall

a way that the main structure of the Museum spans the tent with a clear span of 36 meters. The inner structure of columns, beams, floor, and even a small portion of the arch itself, are to be hung from the main arches once they are in place. They can all be added at the very end of the process, just after tent removal. In effect, the innermost portion of the structure is cantilevered off the great piers that support the arches, and, being prefabricated, can be brought in, and installed, after the arches are in place, once the Museum is sealed and operational.

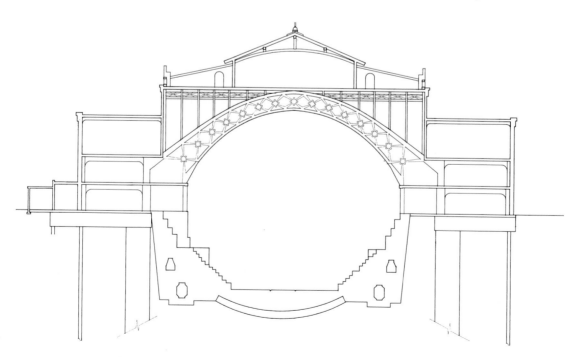

Step 4: Addition of nonstructural finished touches

In the accompanying four drawings we see the sequence of construction operation.

1. The tent in place, as it is today.

2. The new museum structure built over the existing tent, without touching it. This is done using the structural characteristics of the great arch. The main compression forces are in the upper chord of the arch. The lower arch, and the lattice of concrete between the two, work as a stiffener whose presence changes the flexibility of the arch, providing additional structure where required.

The new Museum is now made operational. Air, temperature, and humidity are controlled and brought within limits needed for the conservation process.

3. The tent is removed, while the conservation process now relies on the conditions in the new ship hall.

4. Prefabricated finishing members are brought in by forklift and inserted into position.

Note on over-technical thinking about spanning the tent, which we rejected. At any time in the work required to design the great arches — especially given the extreme difficulty later encountered by the idea of bringing every other arch down on top of a longitudinal arch — it would have been possible to give up and find a purely technical solution. This could most easily have been done by changing the arch shape, and flattening out the ceiling, and using giant lightweight trusses to span the space.

We never gave way to this temptation, simply because the whole interior of the building is posited on the idea of the diamond in its setting. We had determined, with careful experiments on the 1:40 model in our office, that the arch shape drawn earlier is the right setting for the Mary Rose, *and that this shape, and no other we were able to find, does the best job of showing the ship in a harmonious and beautiful fashion.*

If we had succumbed to the difficulty of structural design, and changed over to some other system, or to some other super-technical solution, the structural problem could have been solved more easily. But the whole purpose of the building — to show off the Mary Rose, *as a diamond, to the best possible advantage — would have been undermined. We have chosen a difficult route, but a route that will make the most of the magnificent ship, for a thousand years to come.*

By mid-1992 the design was virtually complete, and had been accepted by the Mary Rose Trust in sufficient detail so that they felt able to send the design out to independent quantity surveyors for a third and independent quantity survey.[12] The results confirmed our previous quantity surveys of £5 million for the shell of the building. It costed out, this time, at £5,036,000.

At this stage, CES had met their brief from the Mary Rose Trust, and the schematic design was approved in all substantive items, including museum layout, exhibit circulation, volume of the ship hall, column spacing, design of arches and structural configuration. At the urging of the Trust and St. James's Palace we were now preparing to submit the building for planning application. But on July 22, before detailed work could continue, the sponsors of the Portsmouth Dockyard who had been expected to underwrite reconstruction of the whole Heritage Area, withdrew their backing for the Dockyard. The construction of the new Museum had to be delayed.

12 Previous estimates had been made in-house by our own organization in California and by PSA-BMSE, our prime consultant in the U.K. Now Mary Rose Trust decided it was time for a fully independent quantity survey, and sent the completed building designs out to Davis Langdon Everest, one of the largest quantity surveyors in England.

CHAPTER FOUR

ACHIEVING A GREAT BUILDING: CONSTRUCTION PROCESS AND COST CONTROL

TO REACH OUR AIMS AND ASPIRATIONS, THIS BUILDING MUST BE BUILT BY ENTIRELY NEW MANAGEMENT TECHNIQUES

The kind of building which the Mary Rose Museum aspires to be is one in which each part is married to the whole, and comes out of the whole—a work standing in the ancient tradition of architecture, but of our time on the threshold of the twenty-first century. Such a building cannot be made from plans drawn by an architect, then simply executed by a building contractor. It must be built by means very different from the means that have been used for building during the last fifty years.

The reason is fundamental. In the evolution of any great work of art, each detail becomes modified by thought, as the building work proceeds. This is what happened to the stone masons who built the great medieval cathedrals. Each stone they carved, was carved in relation to the evolving whole, and therefore took its place correctly.

A NEW APPROACH TO CONSTRUCTION MANAGEMENT

Our experience as contractors, engineers, and architects during the last fifteen years has proved one thing over and over again: the things placed on drawings are inevitably—always—wrong in many particulars. Drawings serve as an important rough sketch of something that will be built, but must be executed with constant attention to room shape, light, wall and ceiling detail, openings—above all to the feelings which arise in each place, in the construction, as it is taking shape. These feelings are too complicated to predict, and *cannot* be predicted. When a building is built from plans that are conceived on the drawing board, and then simply built, the result is sterile at best—silly most of the time—and sometimes unthinkably bad. This is something familiar in virtually all large buildings that have been built since 1950. It is inevitable, given the process of construction used to build them. And it is inevitable that this process must lead to unsatisfactory results.

Recent developments in the construction industry have tended to separate design from construction even further. A process has recently developed where the architect—like a fashion designer dealing with concepts—only sketches the building. That building is then detailed and built by a construction management firm, who create the details in their own offices or using other architects, based on a more solid knowledge of construction process and technique, and then have the building built. The result, of course, is even worse since the building has now been conceived by a fashion designer to whom the fabric and structure of the building is not real.

To build the Mary Rose Museum, we propose to use a form of construction management that is entirely different, one which we have practiced successfully many times over in the United States and in Japan. In this technique, time and cost control are handled by a flexible management team, who have the knowledge, and the authority, to modify the building continuously—with the client's help and knowledge—while keeping the flow of construction and subcontractor operations on target with regard to time and cost.

This technique is not well known in England, although a relative of the CES construction management system does exist there, in a different form, and has been practiced with success by large companies such as Bovis. In these systems, the flexible management is designed for a different purpose: the design is kept constant, while time or cost is reduced. The reduction is achieved by flexible operations which give the managers the chance to make a continuous stream of changes in specifications, details, or scheduling, but

The beauty and delicacy of the massive lightweight structure

always designed to reduce time, or to reduce cost.

The system which we have developed has a similar flexible method of management, and uses very similar techniques, but to achieve very different goals. Again, the specifications, details, and scheduling are changed, while construction is moving forward—and again this is achieved with an experienced team of construction managers, accustomed to flexible operations. However, in the CES system, the goal is different. Our intention is to increase the *quality* of the building, while leaving cost and time unchanged. Thus the savings which are achieved through the use of flexible management

and control over the emerging building, are used to improve *quality* while keeping cost and time fixed.

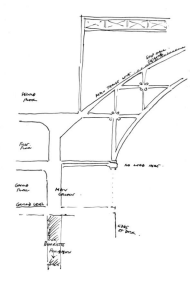

CONSTRUCTION CONTRACTS

The process of construction described in this chapter, and which we contemplate for the Mary Rose Museum, requires an entirely new relation between architect, contractor, and subcontractors, and a new understanding of the relationship between time and flow of money.

The new relation includes the concept that the construction management is headed by the architect, as construction manager. It requires the use of entirely new construction management techniques, and above all, of new contracts. These new contracts address these issues head-on.

For the sake of illustration, at the end of this chapter we reprint two standard contracts currently used by CES in California. They are not the contracts we use for larger jobs, and they will certainly require substantial modification to conform to English legal usage and to English construction practice for the Mary Rose Museum. We print them here because they illustrate, succinctly and clearly, the principles of construction advocated by CES. They describe both the emotional spirit, and the legal essence, of the contracts which we would use in building the Mary Rose Museum.

It may seem unusual to print construction contracts in a book of this type. The mainstream view of architecture to-day ignores the relation of construction management to architecture; treats it as a mundane matter, one of no great importance. It is significant that most students in architecture schools do not study construction contracts; and even on the rare occasions when this might be done it is treated as a boring, practical matter, on a par with having to know something about the way the plumbing works.

Yet the truth is that the contract, which sets out the expectations, conditions, and essence of the bargain which is made with craftspeople to get the building built, has in its fine print, the nature of architecture writ large. The RIBA[13] and AIA[14] contracts in common use today are themselves in large

The entrance ramp passing through the ship hall

Main arches, X-bracing, and longitudinal support arches

13 Royal Institute of British Architects.
14 American Institute of Architects.

Another view of X-bracing and longitudinal arch system

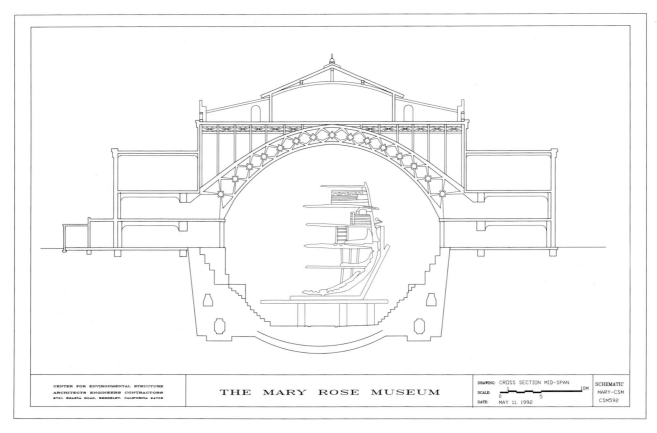

Cross section at the mid-span of the longitudinal arches

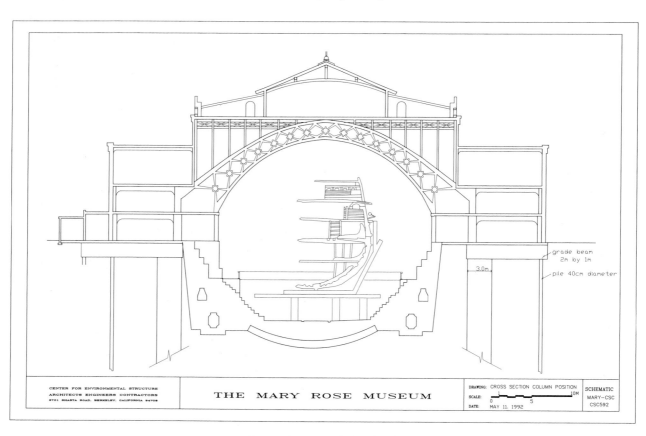

Cross section at a typical major pier

The hull of the Mary Rose *as seen against the arches*

Tracery of the major arch structure

part responsible for the lamentable state of architecture. It is almost true to say that a good building cannot be built within the kind of arrangement contemplated in a "normal" contract.

TIME AND MONEY

Present-day contracts are not only faulty because they take control away from architects and weaken their relation to the evolving building and to the crafts involved. They also all but destroy the building through the system of incentives which they create for the contractor, in regard to time and flow of money.

In the current system, the contractor builds a portion of the building with his own money and receives "draws" once particular phases are complete.[15] This system, ostensibly set up to keep the contractor honest, and to keep the project moving forward, does enormous harm to the building, doesn't benefit the client, and puts the contractor in a state of stress where the only thing he can think about is going as fast as possible in order to invoice the next draw. Under these conditions, where money is used to enforce time constraints, it is impossible to build a profound building.

In the CES system it works differently. We realized long ago that the draw system is a fundamental problem with present-day construction practice that must be solved if "good buildings" are to be built once again. In response, we began a series of experiments with new types of construction management, starting eleven years ago

with one building in Albany, California, in which our construction contract allowed the proper relation between time, money, and incentives to exist on the job. During subsequent years, we have continually evolved our construction contracts to address this problem of money flow, as it relates to time. In these contracts the tasks are broken down into much smaller segments. Where a "typical" contract would call for five draws, our contract has thirty to thirty-five operations, each with its own draws. In addition, the contractor is paid for a portion of the work up front before it is performed, and for the rest of the work as it is performed.

Within any one of the thirty or so operations, the contractor receives 50% of the money for that operation up front, 35% when he has completed about 50 to 60% of the work, and the remaining 15% when that operation is entirely done. The basic principle is that contractors are never working on their own money, and are therefore never rushing to clear a loan. In the case of a retention (normally 10%) they receive 5% upon completion of the operation and 5% on completion of the job.

Under these conditions, the contractor can afford to stop and look around, to begin to understand what is happening to the building, to pay attention to the *needs* of the building as it evolves, and to take care of those needs. Without this modified payment schedule, no amount of goodwill on the part of the contractor can solve the problem, because the money-time relationship will force the contractor

into a situation where he will have to move as fast as possible, and if the building suffers, so be it.

COST ALLOCATION

The driving engine for the new system of management which we use, is a method of cost allocation which *precedes design*. In conventional building design, the architects and engineers design the building, and a cost estimate is then made — in England by a quantity surveyor, in the United States by an estimator. Efforts are then made to reconcile cost overruns with the design, and the design is modified. It is always too late in the game.

In the CES management system, the distribution of money is used, from the first day, to drive the design process. Before almost any geometrical conception of the building design is made, the building is designed as a set of numbers, representing dollar amounts. The building is first assigned a target price: the budget. Main categories are then set up, for all capital construction costs, and the target budget is distributed, intuitively, among these amounts. This intuition relies heavily on experience. But even in the very first distribution of funds among different capital cost categories, one already develops a sense of the building. Amounts are distributed to walls, roof, floors, windows, exterior work, interior finishes, and so on. Even in this first crude distribution of money, one senses the nature of the building which is to be made.

---

15 A draw is a designated amount to be received by the contractor after completion of a certain phase of work.

For example, in CES practice for house construction, we almost invariably assign 20% of the budget to exterior works. This means that fully one-fifth of the building cost is to be spent on exterior construction — walls, steps, trellises, seats, and so on, thus forming a zone of carefully tended construction around the house, which extends the cared-for environment far beyond the building itself. Experience shows that this always pays off, and enlarges the valuable environment of the house. But it has to be paid for. By comparison with a conventional approach in which perhaps 5% might be assigned to landscape, this assignation of 20% reduces the house "itself" from 95% (100% minus 5% in conventional practice) to 80% (100% minus 20% in CES practice). Immediately one has a sense of the way that the distribution of money is working, and how it is defining and affecting the environment.

In the same way, to a practiced eye, this allocation of funds to the building and its elements, gives a complete picture of the design, in its essence, long before the building has even been conceived in plan or in volume. It is the most essential phase in the building process.

On this page and the next we show sample budget allocation sheets of this kind which we made for the Mary Rose Museum long before it was designed.

COST CONTROL DURING DESIGN AND CONSTRUCTION

The overall cost allocation picture becomes the channel through which the design is continually reprocessed, thus keeping each part of the building on budget, both during design, and during construction.

Once the cost allocation has been defined, we use it as a basis for making decisions about design. The essence of the process we follow is that we do not allow cost overruns in one category to reduce costs in another, since this would almost always sacrifice the quality of the building.

To go on with the example of the 20% allocation to exterior

COST ALLOCATIONS FOR MUSEUM AND VICTORY ARENA, FULLY FITTED OUT		
CATEGORY	COST	TOTALS
BUILDING SHELL		
Foundations and slabs	£ 736,000	
Main structure	3,811,000	
Additional shell items	432,000	
SUBTOTAL	4,979,000	£4,979,000
MUSEUM FITTING OUT AND FINISHES		
Mechanical systems	1,020,000	
Finishes	756,000	
Ship hall interior	276,000	
Exhibit interior	1,633,000	
Other interiors	263,000	
SUBTOTAL	3,948,000	£3,948,000
SPECIAL EXHIBIT		
Ship model, pond, wind tunnel	664,000	
SUBTOTAL	664,000	£664,000
RESTAURANT AND SHOP INTERIORS		
Restaurant and shop interiors	566,000	
SUBTOTAL	566,000	£566,000
VICTORY PLAZA		
Victory Plaza	1,043,000	
SUBTOTAL	1,043,000	£1,043,000
GRAND TOTAL		£11,200,000

COST ALLOCATIONS FOR BUILDING SHELL

CATEGORY	UNIT	UNIT PRICE	COST
MAIN STRUCTURE			
Main arch trusses	11	50,000	550,000
Truss arch bracing	10 bays	17,000	170,000
Columns	247	200	49,400
Vaults	2,416 m²	200/m²	483,200
Tent rehang from trusses	1 allow	15,000	15,000
Purlins	1,030 m	15/m	15,450
Load-bearing walls	4,467 m²	140/m²	625,380
Upper level			
structural slab floors	3,934 m²	100/m²	393,400
Flat roof structure	2,580 m²	70/m²	180,600
Pitched roof structure	2,121 m²	75/m²	159,075
Pitched roof surface	2,121 m²	30/m²	63,630
Flat roof surface	2,580 m²	20/m²	51,600
Restaurant trusses and buttresses	11	6,000 ea	66,000
			2,822,735
Contingency	15%	2,822,735	432,410
Management	20%	2,822,735	564,547
SUBTOTAL			£3,819,692
FOUNDATION AND SLABS			
Demolition	1 allow	20,000	20,000
Drilling and piers			
vertical piers	101	1,000 ea	101,000
Drilling and piers			
battered piers	72	2,000 ea	144,000
Grade bms 90 cm by 60 cm by			
total length 1,552 m	838 cm	130/cm	108,940
Slabs on grade, 30 cm	535 cm	100 cm	53,500
Other ground floor slabs	1,283 m²	80/m²	102,640
Tie beams, steel	104 m	150 m	15,600
			545,680
Contingency	15%	545,680	81,852
Management	20%	545,680	109,136
SUBTOTAL			£736,668
ADDITIONAL SHELL ITEMS			
Exterior windows	446 m²	120/m²	53,520
Interior windows	500 m²	120/m²	60,000
Doors	50 drs	150/dr	7,500
Arcade ramp	240 m²	250/m²	60,000
Elevators	4	20,000 ea	80,000
Stairs/ramps	18 flights	3,000/fl	54,000
North balcony	1 allow	5,000	5,000
			320,020
Contingency	15%	320,020	48,000
Management	20%	320,020	64,000
SUBTOTAL			£432,020
GRAND TOTAL FOR SHELL			£4,979,380

construction of a house. It can very often happen, during early planning stages, that certain items within the house begin to go over cost: the client wants expensive built-ins, for example, or beautiful windows. Since such items cannot be contained within the budget which has been set for them, the proposal may often be made, even at that early stage: "let's have the beautiful windows, sacrifice the exterior work—and we'll build that later," (typically the client speaking).

We almost always resist this suggestion. If the building is built without the all-important exterior space, it will be damaged materially. We typically therefore insist that the reduction be made in a cost category which is more closely related to the items which are running over—roof material perhaps, interior finishes, bathroom fixtures, or something else which can be sacrificed. But of course *something* really has to be sacrificed. To pay for one item, another has to disappear or be reduced. That means, very early on, the client begins to appreciate that, to pay for some luxurious item, other items must be rough. Great buildings always have some luxury, and some roughness. The money must be distributed so that some areas are intensified, receive a little more care, are made more beautiful. As a result, less money will be spent on other areas. But this is not a bad thing. It is a good thing because—as in the Alhambra[16]—the reduced areas provide a necessary counterpoint to

the intense areas, allowing them to shine.

This fact too, must be faced squarely, in the cost-cutting measures that are taken. And they must be taken, without sacrificing the values inherent in the cost allocation picture *as a whole*. What is vital, at every stage, is that the importance of one item is not allowed to upset the building as a whole, by damaging some other item which is essential to the feeling of the building as a whole. At all events, we try to keep the overall balance intact.

Let us consider an example, previously mentioned, from the early design stage of the Mary Rose Museum, with respect to the foundation. Our cost allocation for this item was £548,000 ($932,000). The best estimate for this work after months of work was £800,000, down from an earlier estimate of over £1 million. If we had stopped at this point and decided that we had done well enough, we would have had to take £252,000 ($428,000) from some other item. Instinct told us that the great arches themselves were threatened. If we allowed the foundation to cost £800,000 ($1.36 million), then the arches and the beauty of the structure would have been threatened, possibly lost altogether. It was therefore vital for the good of the building as a whole, that we could leave the other structural items in the cost allocation intact. This meant the foundation problem *had* to be solved: in other words, we *had* to find a structurally acceptable founda-

tion for the £548,000, and not a penny more. The way in which this was finally accomplished is described under the foundation section.[17] But what is essential here is to show the attitude which goes with the cost allocation method. It is an attitude which focusses attention, at every stage, on the beauty of the building as a whole, and keeps every decision moving in the direction mandated by that concern for balance.

The same thing happens, of course, during the construction phase itself. As construction moves forward, some items cost less than expected, others cost more than expected. Once again, we do not allow items in the "more than expected" category to produce a cost overrun. Instead measures are taken, dynamically, during the construction process. Either quantities are reduced—if that is feasible, to make up for the overrun—or items are reduced, simplified, in other areas of the building—always with an eye to preserving the feeling of the building as a whole, and its essential character. This guarantees cost, in a form rarely accomplished by contemporary architecture.

But it requires a great deal of creative energy. The allocation and redistribution is a creative process, which demands time, skill, and effort, from the construction manager on site and from the architect. These are not details to be "left to the contractor." They are issues which require the full design experience of the engineers and architects

16 Granada, 14th century. In Moorish Spain the idea of a proper balance of rough and smooth was commonplace.
17 See pages 53–55.

who made the design initially. And this is why, in the CES management process, the same team of designers and managers are involved, from the beginning of the design work to the end of construction.

In the CES method, the use of money is a creative act, on par with the architect's sketching, and it has the result that if any one item were to change in cost, the results would ripple throughout the entire project, forcing changes in other items. To a trained person the cost allocation sheets, almost never more than a couple of pages long, completely describe the building in many ways more completely than the design drawings. The allocations tell you where the money is being spent, what the special items are, and where the building will have a "rougher" character. For these reasons, designing the building so that every item meets its cost allocation amount is taken as a deadly serious matter, and much of the design work is directed towards that end.

CRAFTSMEN AND SUBCONTRACTORS

The heart of the process by which we intend to build this building relies on a form of management, and a form of contract, in which decisions are being made directly, by the design and architectural and building team, throughout construction.

In this process, it is our intention to work directly with the subcontractors. In present British practice the word "subcontractor" has often come to mean just another giant construction company. Indeed, when we first spoke with our colleagues in

Portsmouth about this project, we heard to our astonishment that a British norm for a £10 million construction project like this one would be to have no more than four or five subcontractors.

We made it clear, very quickly, to our Portsmouth colleagues that something entirely different would be needed, and that we have a tradition of working in detail, very closely, with the actual men and women who are doing the work. Our guess is that on this job, we would have some fifty subcontractors.

Our own managers, experienced in this type of work, will run the individual craftspeople directly. We will have a group doing concrete, a group doing stone, a group doing brickwork, craftspeople making and setting tile, individual subs doing ironwork, individuals doing rough carpentry, another group doing cabinetwork, others doing plaster.

In all of this, it is the individual plasterers, bricklayers, formwork-carpenters, who make the difference. And the way the operation is run requires that the details of their work can be planned flexibly, and that changes and subtleties are being worked out continuously, between our team of managers and the craftspeople, while the work is going on.

It is only this approach which allows the building to take on the character it *has* to have if it is to have true life as a building. One simply cannot predict, accurately, what it will take to make the building harmonious, when everything has to be thought out in advance. The detail of a railing, the exact position of the windows, the subdivision of these windows,

the shape of column capitals, the pattern of floor work, the exact height of low walls and balustrades, the precise width and position of a doorway, the source and intensity of light, the color and finish of an interior wall, the amount of extra detail in the entrance of the building, the amount of shade and sunshine — these are the details which ultimately govern the harmony and depth of the building. They can only come from careful, day-by-day examination of these details while they are being built, in place, together with the actual individuals who are doing the work.

It is for this reason that we always work directly with our subcontractors and craftspeople, and it is for this reason that we have them working for *us* — not for a mechanized, computerized general contractor that stands in between.

TECHNIQUES OF CONSTRUCTION

Just as new forms of management are needed to produce life in a building, so these must be complemented by new forms of construction technique that are suited to the creation of the forms. To make the construction process well adapted to the beauty of the building, to keep the work on budget and to build structures that have a "reality" to them — that is, structures built of real materials and in configurations which make sense of the materials — it is necessary to be inventive in the detailed specifications of construction sequence and methods.

This concern is different from concerns about contract management — but deeply related, because it also affects se-

Dining hall trusses of similar construction, San Jose, California, 1989

quence and process in ways that have to do with *feeling*. This is vastly different from today's widespread interest in construction processes invented purely for efficiency.

As an example, consider the erection and fabrication of the Museum's arches. When we first began thinking about the concrete lacework arches, we intended to build them by shooting them with gunite (high-strength, dry sand concrete shot under pressure). Other arches built by this method are illustrated on this page, where we show a series of a similar, but smaller lacework arches recently built for a public building in California. In this building the lightweight forms, and steel, were suspended in mid-air in the position they were going to occupy, and the gunite

was then shot directly into the forms.

After careful thought about staging of construction for the Museum and about the finish on the arches, we decided that different methods of construction would work better for the Museum arches. We show the gunite arches, however, to make it clear that even the highly intricate geometrical structures of the Museum arches can be built, with little extra cost, provided that construction conditions and construction methods are solved with inventiveness.

For the Mary Rose Museum, our gunite technique has two disadvantages. First, the complex operation over the dock might endanger the ship, and might also be potentially dangerous for the gunite crews. Second, the surface of the shot

concrete, even when "struck off," would be rough, and might not easily meet the demands for a smooth, nonporous surface required for easy cleaning.

We have therefore devised a different erection procedure, in which the arches are to be cast on the ground as cast-stone or cast concrete in three sections, and then raised into position from travelling cranes running on rails along the two sides of the dock.

This technique has been studied thoroughly at the first level of detail, and has been estimated to our predicted figure of £550,000 ($935,000) for eleven arches by a British subcontractor.

Other parts of the building will need equally inventive approaches to construction and fabrication. Each technique must allow its material to be formed and worked to produce feeling and substance in the building, without unusual cost.

SAMPLE CONSTRUCTION CONTRACTS

The following contracts are printed here because they are meant to suggest, to indicate, an entirely different attitude to the task of construction; and to suggest that this new attitude is not merely something to dream about. It is a practical matter, which, by appropriate practical devices, including new forms of contract, *can* be brought about.

Although some of the people involved in planning the Museum found the concept of the new contracting arrangements difficult and perhaps a little alien, we were gratified that the top managers at Bovis and PSA-BMSE, when they studied our proposals, took them very seriously and immediately rec-

ognized the vast shift in idea and process which these contracts signify.

We hope that the Mary Rose Museum will be able to embody the new spirit in architecture, by making use of these construction management techniques and contracts, and that the promise of a new architecture will be made real, exactly by technical and administrative devices such as these.

CONSTRUCTION MANAGEMENT CONTRACT[18]

This contract is made on this _____ day of _____, between _____ (hereinafter called Owner), and the Center for Environmental Structure (CES or Construction Manager and General Contractor of record), for the purpose of building the _____ at _____ location, according to plans prepared by the Center for Environmental Structure.

ARTICLE 1. DEFINITION OF PROJECT
The work is shown on the drawings that are attached to this contract as appendix 1, and specified by the 23 construction operations attached to this contract as subcontract proposals in appendix 2.
The following aspects of the work will be built as specified in the drawings:
a. Siting of the building(s) as shown on the site plan.
b. Configurations and dimensions of building(s) and rooms as shown on floor plan sheets.
c. Additional interior and exterior work determined by CES during construction.
It is understood that the drawings have been obtained for building permit purposes, and are not to be construed as binding architectural plans and specs.

ARTICLE 2. BASE PRICE
Signed subcontract proposals attached in appendix 2 spell out the relative specifications and costs.
Based on these documents, the base price of the building(s) will be $_____, plus whatever changes shall be agreed to by the Owner in writing.

ARTICLE 3. CES RESPONSIBILITY
CES shall provide management services and supervision necessary to execute and complete construction of the project.
CES will, as construction manager,
1. Enter into binding subcontracts with subcontractors.
2. Organize and manage the subcontractors.
3. Make changes to the design.
4. Determine how to spend the available budget so as to most benefit the building(s).
5. Administer construction work so as to meet our understanding of applicable codes.
6. Inspect finished work.
7. Obtain lien releases from subcontractors in exchange for final payment.
8. Keep full and detailed accounts as may be necessary for the construction of the project on behalf of the Owner, and will make those records available to the Owner at any time.
9. At completion, shall provide to the Owner a copy of the marked up job-site drawings, for the Owner's use and records.
In all matters of subcontractor dealings, in all matters of design changes, and in all matters of money management, the Owner grants CES complete authority to exercise its judgment on behalf of the Owner.

ARTICLE 4. CES GENERAL PHILOSOPHY
It is believed that the approach to construction laid out in this contract and based on the fundamental assumptions above will secure for the Owner the highest quality building(s) possible within the available budget.

---

18 This general management contract and the following subcontract were developed from 1983 to 1994 by Christopher Alexander, Gary Black, and James Maguire of CES, and the authors gratefully acknowledge James Maguire's contribution to this work.

Specifically, this approach is designed to eliminate the profit motive of the general contractor. By setting a fixed fee for the management of the job and maintaining open records of all transactions, the typical overbidding by the contractor to protect himself from unforeseen overruns and contractor's markups on materials and subcontracted work are eliminated. In the typical owner-contractor arrangement the overbid money becomes windfall for the contractor and does not benefit the building(s) or the owner. In the model laid out in this contract all available money is spent for the betterment of the building(s).

This method also provides the framework for efficiently dealing with changes which are a fundamental part of making a good building. In the typical Owner-Contractor agreement any changes are discouraged by adding an exorbitant surcharge to the direct costs of the changes, effectively providing the contractor a windfall profit. Even changes which reduce the costs are typically charged as extras. In the method laid out here changes are not subject to additional surcharges and are charged at their actual costs.

CES encourages the Owner to review all subcontracts, and to propose alternative lower-priced subcontractors. CES will evaluate the subcontractor proposals and award subcontracts if CES determines that it is in the best interest of the project, and provided that these proposals are consistent with the construction schedule.

ARTICLE 5. SUMMARY OF CONSTRUCTION OPERATIONS

The construction will be organized under the following construction operations, with the following sums allocated to them. Detailed break-down, showing subcontract amount, 15% contingency, and CES management fee is given in appendix 3.

1. GENERAL CONDITIONS	————	13. PLUMBING	————
2. FOUNDATIONS	————	14. ELECTRICAL	————
3. FRAME	————	15. HVAC	————
4. FLOOR STRUCTURE	————	16. ROADS AND PARKING	————
5. ROOF STRUCTURE	————	17. CIVIL WORKS	————
6. EXTERIOR WALLS	————	18. INTERIOR FINISH WORK	————
7. INTERIOR WALLS	————	19. CABINETWORK AND FURNISHINGS	————
8. ROOFING	————	20. PAINTWORK	————
9. MISC. METAL	————	21. GARDENS AND LANDSCAPE	————
10. WINDOWS/DOORS	————	22. OWNER'S REQUESTS	————
11. BRICK AND TILE	————	23. BIDDING FEE	————
12. PLASTERWORK	————		

TOTAL BUDGET ————

The total dollar amount under subcontractor's subcontract proposals and the total dollar amount under contingency will be used by CES to build the building(s). The use of this money is under the sole discretion of CES acting as the manager for the Owner, and may be applied to cost overruns or for any items required by CES to improve or upgrade the building(s).

ARTICLE 6. MANAGEMENT FEE

The Management Fees will be paid directly to CES as outlined under Article 9. The management fees will be used by CES to manage the project and will pay for CES management labor and overheads.

The total management fee paid to CES is $———— plus 20% of construction for all construction above $————.

The portion of this fee paid to CES for managing the construction of the project as outlined in this contract will be $———— plus 16% of construction for all construction above $————. This sum will be paid to CES according to the arrangement described in article 9.

The remaining portion of the fee ($———— plus 4% of construction for all construction above $————) will be paid to CES to cover bidding, organization of subcontractors and setup: $———— to be paid as a lump sum, on notification by CES that the bidding work has begun; the remaining $———— plus 4% to be paid on completion of the setup work.

ARTICLE 7. ALLOWANCES

Allowances are included in the main contract and subcontract documents for certain items not specified in detail. This portion of the budget is to be used by the Owner. The Owner can spend up to the allowance amount. If the Owner spends less than the allowance amount, the Owner will have the option of applying the savings to other allowance items. If the Owner wishes to spend more than the allowance amount, then they must spend less on subsequent allowance items or supply additional funds.

ARTICLE 8. CONTINGENCY

To protect the Owner and the job against unforeseeable fluctuations of price, unforeseen site conditions, and other changes, each of the budgeted amounts in article 5 contains a contingency of 15%. The contingency money is to be used entirely at CES discretion, for the benefit of the building(s) as judged by CES. CES shall have the right to distribute and redistribute this contingency money as it sees fit, in order to meet difficulties and changes which arise in the building(s), and whenever possible, to make improvements and extras which CES believes will increase the harmony of the emerging building(s).

CES's intention is to maintain as much of the 15% contingency money as possible, and use this money to pay craftsmen who will make various finishing touches continuously throughout the job.

ARTICLE 9. PAYMENT PROCEDURE

The Owner will open a project checking account and make deposits to the account according to the schedule below. CES will be signatory on this account, and will have control of the project checkbook.

The basis for payment will be the list of Construction Operations. Summary in article 5 and detail in appendix 3.

The Owner will make deposits to the project checking account according to the following schedule for each operation:

50% of the price of the operation will be deposited to the account upon notification of the commencement of that operation.

35% of the price of the operation, on demand, when a reasonable portion of the work is completed.

10% of the price of the operation when notified by CES that the operation is at least 85% complete.

The remaining 5% will be paid according to the provisions of article 14.

As each check is deposited to the account, CES will withdraw the appropriate amount from the management category (as shown in appendix 3) to make payment for construction management fees, up to 95% of the total management fee. The remaining 5% of the total management fee will be deposited to CES upon final completion.

All records from the project account and all invoices for materials and labor, and all subcontractor's billings will be available for the Owner's review.

ARTICLE 10. SUBCONTRACTORS

Subcontract proposals for items 2–21 are attached as appendix 2. These proposals, signed by the various subcontractors constitute an addendum to the general contract, and serve as the basis for the project specifications and the construction budget. At the appropriate time CES will obtain subcontract proposals from subcontractors for any remaining items.

In performance of this task, CES will seek out and hire subcontractors which in CES's opinion are most appropriate for the particular job. The criteria may be price in one instance, timeliness in another, and quality of work in another. CES is under no obligation to find the "lowest" subcontractor, nor the "best" subcontractor.

Should a subcontractor default on their subcontract, for any reason, CES will endeavor to renegotiate or find another subcontractor to perform the work. CES will proceed in a manner which it determines is in the best interests of the Owner and the project with respect to time, quality, flexibility, and price, but CES is under no obligation to provide subcontracts or subcontractors at a guaranteed price.

The relationship between CES and the subcontractors shall be a contractor-subcontractor relationship. Within the confines of such a relationship, CES will include its best efforts to provide appropriate guidance of the subcontractors in the performance of their work. CES is to be sole agent on behalf of the Owner. The Owner or any agents of the Owner aside from CES, are explicitly forbidden from giving any directions to, or making any requests directly to any of the subcontractors. The Owner may, of course, make requests through CES as provided in article 11.

ARTICLE 11. DESIGN DECISIONS AND CHANGES INITIATED BY CES

Part of CES philosophy is that there are no defined plans and specifications. CES will have authority to make design decisions and design changes as it determines necessary, without written confirmation from the Owner, as long as these decisions do not increase the total budgeted cost. Whenever possible CES will confer with the Owner but CES is not obligated to do so. Design decisions and changes may be generated by any of the following causes.

CES-initiated design changes may be generated in response to the emerging building(s). As the building(s) and rooms begin to take shape, doorway sizes and locations, window sizes and locations, wall locations and wall lengths, cabinets, finishes, etc. may have to be altered. These decisions can only be made on the site, during construction, as the building(s) is taking shape.

CES-initiated design changes will be required to keep the overall price of the building(s) in budget. As a result of some unforeseeable problem, or as a result of an overage due to a previous design change, it will become necessary to make changes in the building(s) to offset the overages. This is not something that might *happen, it is something that* will *happen. Although often seen as negative, these types of changes are more often than not positive changes which ultimately result in producing the best buildings.*

CES will confer with the Owner in major design decisions which the Owner has identified as important ahead of time, and before making any major design changes, but CES has the main commitment to "listen" to the emerging building(s), and to do what is in the best interests of the building(s). The Owner will be consulted on and encouraged to participate in the detailed layout of _____ as the Owner has requested.

ARTICLE 12. CHANGES NOT COVERED BY ARTICLE 11.

Changes not covered by article 11, and resulting in an increase of cost, will be approved in writing by the Owner. In cases where an increase of cost is anticipated, the Owner must approve the change in writing before CES can begin the work. If the Owner does not approve it, the work will not be done.

ARTICLE 13. TIME

The work to be performed under this contract shall commence within 15 days of the signing of this contract. The work shall be completed in accordance with the schedule provided pursuant to the paragraph below.

Both Owner and CES desire to complete the project in _____ months starting from the date of commencement. CES will provide the Owner with an estimated construction schedule for the project. This schedule shall indicate the dates for the starting and completion of the various stages of the construction and shall contain the necessary information to allow the Owner to monitor the progress of the work. It shall be revised as required by the conditions of the work and those conditions and events which are beyond the control of CES.

The Owner agrees that if the building process is slowed down, by any act or neglect of Owner, by any separate contractor employed by the Owner, by any unreasonably slow process of decision making or design negotiation from the Owner, CES will then be entitled to an appropriate increase of management fee, to make up for the extra time. If the building process is slowed down for any other reason not caused by CES negligence, CES and the Owner will negotiate fair compensation if any additional management fee is required. Adherence to time conditions is of vital importance to the proper running of the job site, and is of material importance to the successful completion of this contract.

ARTICLE 14. SUBSTANTIAL COMPLETION

The date of substantial completion of the project or a designated portion thereof is the date when construction is sufficiently complete in accordance with the drawings and specifications so the Owner can occupy or utilize or, in fact, does occupy or utilize, the project or designated portion thereof for the use for which it is intended.

The date of substantial completion shall be established in writing, signed by the Owner and CES. At that time, a punch list of items to be completed or corrected (if any) shall be prepared by the Owner and CES along with a time schedule for their completion or correction, and the remaining unpaid balance of the contract including the 5% subcontract retentions will be deposited to the construction account.

ARTICLE 15. LIEN RELEASES

CES warrants that all money paid by Owner, except management, will be used on the building to pay for materials, job expenses, subcontractors and craftsmen.

CES will obtain partial waivers of lien for all payments to subcontractors and will forward these to the Owner.

ARTICLE 16. FINAL PAYMENT

Following full completion of the work as defined by the punch list (article 14) and final inspection and acceptance of the work in writing by the Owner, CES shall have authority to make final payments to subcontractors, and to withdraw final payment of the management fee. To protect the Owner CES agrees that they will not use these funds to make final payments until the subcontractor has provided the appropriate final lien releases. When all payments have been made, CES will issue a duly executed final waiver of lien.

ARTICLE 17. CES OBLIGATION AND FIRST-YEAR REPAIRS

CES will maintain $_____ from the contingency in the job account, for a period of one year after final completion. This money is to be spent for repairs and annoyance items which occur after final completion. CES will use the $_____ at its discretion, to fix items that are unsatisfactory to the Owner. If, one year after final completion, this money or any part of it remains unspent, CES will use the balance in consultation with the Owner, to make some nice small improvements to the building(s). CES shall have no further obligation, beyond that covered by this money, for making repairs or improvements on items considered unsatisfactory by the Owner. CES will also make its best efforts to help the Owner enforce the warranties provided by subcontractors.

ARTICLE 18. JOB EXPENSES

Owner will maintain working telephones on site at all times. Owner will supply working electric service and water to the job site. Owner will supply toilet, storage, cleanup facilities and lunch room for subcontractors workers at all times. Owner will reimburse CES management personnel for mileage to and from CES office, at 27 cents per mile. CES will pay the phone, electric, water and toilet bills, together with mileage reimbursements out of the job account. Estimated costs for these items are included in the construction budget under general conditions. If these costs run above estimate, overage is to be carried by Owner.

ARTICLE 19. UNKNOWN CONDITIONS

The work may include modification or connection to existing structures. It is not possible to anticipate all problems which may arise, in the work of connecting to such existing structures. If unexpected conditions that affect the performance of the work and vary from those indicated by the contract documents, are encountered, base price of project and schedule shall be equitably adjusted for such unexpected conditions in writing between CES and the Owner upon claim made by CES.

ARTICLE 20. INSURANCE

The Owner will carry all necessary general liability, fire, and earthquake insurance and any other insurance which may be required to protect the Owner against claims which may arise from operations under this project.

CES will purchase and maintain the following insurance to cover CES's operations under this agreement:

1. Worker's compensation insurance in full compliance with worker's compensation laws of the State of California for all employees of CES and other persons directly associated with CES's management team.

2. CES will, in addition, request that all subcontractors provide certificates of worker's compensation insurance for their employees. In any case where this is unavailable, CES will carry the necessary worker's compensation on its own policy and deduct the cost from the subcontract price.

ARTICLE 21. CES SPECIAL CONSTRUCTION METHODS AND PHILOSOPHY

The Owner recognizes that the methods and philosophy of CES include unusual use of materials, and unusual combinations of high-level and low-level finish. The building(s) will not necessarily be designed to typical California industry standards for residential or public buildings, and the Owner's desire to break with these prevailing standards is explicitly part of the intent of this contract.

Owner approves the form and content of the CES subcontract forms attached to this contract as appendix 2, and recognizes the right of CES to make substitutions as provided in the subcontract agreements.

The Owner is specifically bargaining for CES's exercise of its independent judgment in carrying out the above-described construction methods and philosophy.

ARTICLE 22. SAFETY

CES shall take necessary precautions for the safety of CES employees on the job, and shall comply with all applicable provisions of federal, state and municipal safety laws. CES shall have no responsibility for the abatement of safety hazards resulting from work at the job site carried on by other persons, or by subcontractors. Subcontractors will be responsible for their own safety, but CES and CES employees will encourage safety on the site.

ARTICLE 23. WARRANTIES

CES warrants to the Owner that all materials and equipment furnished under this agreement will be new unless otherwise specified, and that all construction work will be of good quality, free from improper workmanship and defective materials. Any warranty or guarantee obtained by CES from any manufacturer, shall be deemed to have been obtained for the benefit of the Owner. CES will collect all equipment manuals and deliver them to the Owner together with all written warranties from equipment manufacturers, and CES will have no further obligation with respect to them.

ARTICLE 24. ATTACHMENTS

The signed subcontracts and documents attached hereto as appendices are expressly incorporated into this contract. To the extent the attachments are inconsistent with the main contract, the terms of the main contract shall govern.

ARTICLE 25. ARBITRATION

Claims, disputes and other matters in question between the parties to this agreement arising out of or relating to the agreement shall be decided by arbitration in accordance with the construction industry arbitration rules of the American Arbitration Association then in effect, unless the parties agree otherwise. This provision shall be specifically enforceable in any court of competent jurisdiction.

Notice of demand for arbitration shall be filed in writing with the other party to this agreement and with the American Arbitration Association. The demand shall be made within a reasonable time after the claim, dispute or other matter in question has arisen. In no event shall the demand for arbitration be made after the date when the applicable statute of limitations would bar institution of a legal or equitable proceeding based on such claim, dispute or other matter in question.

The award rendered by arbitrators shall be final, and judgment may be entered upon it in accordance with applicable law in any court having jurisdiction.

Unless otherwise agreed in writing, CES shall carry on the work and maintain its progress during any arbitration proceedings, and the Owner shall continue to make payments to CES in accordance with the contract documents.

This article shall survive completion or termination of this agreement.

ARTICLE 26. ATTORNEYS' FEES

In the event that either party files suit to enforce the provisions of this contract, the prevailing party shall be entitled to a reasonable attorney's fee as cost of suit, to be fixed by the Court.

Signed

_____   _____
for the Owner   date   for CES   date

CRAFTSMAN/SUBCONTRACTOR AGREEMENT

This agreement seeks to obtain the best possible work for the owner by obtaining design and construction input from the craftsman, encouraging an old-world attitude of quality towards the work, and by giving flexibility of on-site design decisions to CES. This agreement is made on this _____ day of _____, 19__, between The Center for Environmental Structure (hereinafter CES) and the craftsman defined below (hereinafter craftsman). All subcontractors are referred to as craftsman, even when a company or organization is providing service, and even in the case of heavy engineering works, in order to emphasize the craft-like nature of the work which CES expects.

CRAFTSMAN/SUBCONTRACTOR

_____

JOB DESCRIPTION

_____

For details of job description see page 3 of this contract.

PRICE _____

PART 1
GENERAL CONDITIONS

ARTICLE 1. PURPOSE

The purpose of the work is to build a building under conditions which allow craft, care, love of the building(s), love of work, and the life of the emerging building(s), to be created to the maximum extent possible. The nature of this subcontract is designed to make this possible, while protecting the interests of owner, manager and craftsman.

ARTICLE 2. DEFINITION OF THE WORK

The craftsman will perform the work defined in the job description attached to this contract, and signed and dated by the parties. It is agreed that this work is defined and modified by the conditions of part 2, articles 7–11.

ARTICLE 3. PRICE AND PAYMENT SCHEDULE

For performing the work specified in article 2, the craftsman will be paid a total price of $_____.
The first 80% of the price will be paid to the craftsman in progress payments based on percentage of work completed, as approved by CES.
15% of the price will be paid to the craftsman after completion of the craftsman's work, and after written declaration by CES that the work is satisfactory and complete.
The final 5% of the price will be paid to the craftsman after final completion of the construction contract, and after sign-off of the punch list by the owner.

ARTICLE 4. CRAFTSMAN RESPONSIBILITIES

The craftsman is responsible for:

1) Insuring compliance with applicable codes.

2) Adhering unequivocally to the price set forth in this contract.

3) Following good construction practice.

4) Either 4a or 4b. One must be checked.

4a) Providing affidavits of worker's compensation insurance. ____

4b) Making provision to be carried on CES's worker's compensation insurance. ____

5) Providing the owner with a completed package as set forth in article 5.

6) All penetration of building components shall be neat, sleeved, and fire-stopped and shall not compromise structural integrity or water-tightness of the structure.

7) Craftsman will clean up all dirt, blemishes and trash generated by his job, and haul away, leaving the site clean of his work.

8) Craftsman will come back to repair or modify any items not adequately completed, at the direction of CES when final punch list is made between CES and owner.

ARTICLE 5. CRAFTSMAN'S GOAL

The ultimate purpose of this agreement is to secure the craftsman's work under conditions which make the craftsman's work a work of beauty and pride and self-respect, and in which the craftsman leaves behind work he is proud of, and can cherish in the future.

It is specifically understood that the craftsman's goal is not only to be paid for his work, but that the beauty and satisfaction of the work itself provide part of the craftsman's reward. To this end, the craftsman shall be treated as an artist who has some power and control over his work as necessary to allow the creation of a beautiful and fitting work within limits accepted by CES.

ARTICLE 6. GUARANTEE

Craftsman warranties his work for a period of _____ *and will repair or replace any item found defective within the warranty period.*

PART 2
RULES GOVERNING EVOLUTION OF THE WORK

ARTICLE 7. BASIC RULE

The essential agreement governing this contract, is that the price remains fixed, and that changes made by CES or by the craftsman, are always made while keeping the price fixed.

ARTICLE 8. CRAFTSMAN'S OWN TIME FOR BEAUTIFUL EXTRAS

It is explicitly present in this agreement that in performance of article 5 (part 1), the craftsman will spend some time over and beyond the call of duty, to make a few very nice details. The craftsman will choose the time, location and nature of these details, and will do them with the intent to make a good job of the project. These details should be checked with CES manager before performance.

ARTICLE 9. EXTRA LABOR AND MATERIALS ALLOWANCE UNDER CES CONTROL

As part of the performance of this contract the craftsman will provide _____ *crew-days of labor and a* _____ *materials allowance to undertake any extras directed by CES. A crew is* _____.

These extras are specifically over and above the performance of the base task defined in the job description, and are intended to provide small extras which will make the job better and more beautiful.

ARTICLE 10. SUBSTITUTIONS

CES shall have the right to make substitutions within the basic job description, reducing some portion of the work, to pay for an increase in other portions. Substitutions are to be negotiated with craftsman, and not to increase total price.

ARTICLE 11. FLEXIBILITY DURING CONSTRUCTION

There is an essential base condition to this contract: In order to make the best building(s) possible, it is not always possible to define the work exactly, ahead of time. The use of working drawings as a precise determination of construction responsibility does not allow the proper life to appear in the building(s), and is specifically eschewed by this agreement. The purpose of this agreement is to give CES and the craftsman the necessary flexibility during construction, while protecting the owner in regard to price.

In order to protect the owner from unacceptable cost overruns, the parties have agreed that the work will be done for a fixed budget, and that the owner will have the work specified in this subcontract performed for a definite fixed sum.

In order to protect the craftsman from having to perform more than he can fairly do under the fixed-sum contract, the craftsman has the right to rearrange the work after negotiation with CES. When CES makes requests not covered or anticipated in the job description, and which clearly cost more, CES and craftsman will then negotiate to reduce work or material or labor in one portion of the subcontract, to make up for the new needs. The owner accepts this arrangement as the necessary consequence of a more flexible approach to building, and a fixed-price contract. It means that some items may be built to a reduced specification or not built at all.

The essential purpose of this contract, is to produce a fair and balanced solution of this base condition, in a way which is fair to all parties. It must be emphasized that all parties, CES, owner and subcontractor, have an interest in making sure that this condition is fairly met. The parties agree to this condition and accept it as essential to all performance of the work.

PART 3
SPECIAL CONDITIONS

ARTICLE 12. SCHEDULE

CES will give craftsman 15 days notice prior to start of job, and craftsman will commence work on the specified day. Work is to be completed within _____ *days thereafter.*

ARTICLE 13. LIEN RELEASES
Craftsman will sign a partial lien release executed with each progress payment.

ARTICLE 14. CHANGES REQUESTED BY CES WHICH REQUIRE ADDITIONAL COMPENSATION
This contract, as written, only covers those items of work defined in the signed job description, or explicitly dealt with under the items of flexibility section (article 5). Items of extra work outside the range of flexibility, which arise as a result of requests made by CES, shall be negotiated and charged separately to the owner.

ARTICLE 15. UNANTICIPATED WORK CAUSED BY UNANTICIPATED CONDITIONS OR OWNER'S REQUESTS
Extra work which arises during performance of the job, whether as a result of unforeseen job conditions or as a result of requests made by the owner, shall be negotiated and charged separately to the owner.

ARTICLE 16. COORDINATION WITH CES REPRESENTATIVE
Craftsman is directly responsible to CES representative only, and may not act upon requests made by the owner, unless these are channeled through CES.

Signed

_____   *date*   *for CES*   _____   *date*
Craftsman/Subcontractor

JOB DESCRIPTION
The description below gives our current understanding of the particulars for the _____ *job for the* _____ *building(s).*

On top of base job, job price must also include _____ *crew-days of labor under CES control, for architectural extras to be defined by CES.*

TIMING
Work to be done between _____ .

SUBCONTRACT PROPOSAL REQUEST
The enclosed documents show our current understanding of the _____ *job for the* _____ *building(s).*
The maximum amount allocated for this item is $ _____ . *It is imperative that you make a proposal which is less than or equal to this amount. If you cannot meet this budget or better it, you may propose a reduction of scope or change of specifications.*
Please submit a detailed proposal for this job on page 3 of our enclosed subcontract forms. We shall award this contract to the subcontractor who defines the most attractive proposal. We strongly recommend that you discuss with us, and negotiate in detail, the nature of your proposal, before making your written submission.

COMPLETENESS OF PROPOSAL
This list may not be complete. It is the craftsman's responsibility to study the _____ *job in detail, and to include in his proposal everything necessary to do a complete job.*

PSA-BMSE[19]/BOVIS[20] ANALYSIS OF CES MANAGEMENT TECHNIQUES

At the suggestion of the Prince of Wales, in early 1992, we asked PSA-BMSE in Portsmouth, in conjunction with their contractor-manager Bovis, the British construction consortium, to make an assessment of the Museum's feasibility — both with regard to engineering and construction techniques, and with regard to the all-important question of construction management as it has been described in the foregoing pages. We sought advice in particular, as to the British firm's assessment of the suitability of CES management techniques for British conditions, and of the possibility of adapting these techniques to the construction of the Mary Rose Museum. These questions were asked in the context of an overall request to PSA and Bovis to join with us in building the Mary Rose Museum, and

---

19 PSA (Property Services Agency) and its southeast division PSA-BMSE (Building Management South-East) provided us with numerous engineering and management consulting services. John Hewitt, chief engineer of the Portsmouth office, in particular provided a wealth of information and enthusiastic support.
20 Bovis, the construction consortium, was at the time of this work helping to reorganize PSA. In their capacity as contractor manager for PSA, and in view of their vast experience with different forms of construction management, Bovis provided support to the studies which are reported below.

the answers reflect the conviction of these two organizations in their readiness to stand behind the building design, its cost, and the novel management techniques which we proposed to introduce.

The preliminary report, issued by PSA-BMSE and Bovis for CES and for the Prince of Wales, and submitted to Mary Rose Trust in January 1992, concluded with the following lengthy statement:

The CES approach to building design and procurement is fundamentally different, whilst at the same time embodies many aspects of construction practice adopted in the UK. CES proposes, uniquely, that the architect should assume the role of Prime manager of both design and construction, and to implement this approach by the use of specialized forms of management contract and sub-contract.

We have reviewed the methods advocated by CES in the context of more traditional building procurement strategies, but primarily those which take account of the three principal project constraints:

1. The constraint of time imposed on the project.

2. The essential requirement, in our view, to complete overall investigations and design development before proceeding to the working drawing/construction phase.

3. The need to secure planning approval for a coherent building design.

We have mentioned already that we consider it is essential to conclude all fundamental design issues before proceeding to the working drawing/construction phase. This is especially important, in our view, on a project as complex as the Mary Rose Museum. In consequence, we believe that the project strategy should permit adequate pre-construction development time, whilst also incorporating a measure of carefully controlled parallel working, to accommodate the principal constraint imposed by the ship hall completion date.

There are two main approaches to procuring buildings in the UK where speed is of the essence, and some parallel development working is essential:

1. The first, Design and Build, involves an architect in direct contract with a builder, employed by the Client to deliver the building to time and to cost. Whether the same architect is employed throughout the process, from concept to completion is immaterial, the building design depends on commercial considerations.

For routine buildings such as offices and supermarkets where quality and sensitivity of design are subordinate to other factors, this system can be effective. We consider however, that such a procurement method is inappropriate to a building as important as the Mary Rose Museum.

2. The second contractual approach may take one of two forms: Management Contracting, in which the Client enters into separate contracts with a Designer and a Management Contractor. The Management Contractor enters into sub-contracts with Works Contractors.

Construction Management (CM), in which the Client enters into separate contracts with a Designer, a Construction Manager and the Works Contractors.

For a project of the size of the Mary Rose Museum, recent UK research suggests that employment of a Construction Manager is a preferred form of management given the demands of many Clients for the controls inherent in the familiar framework of traditional contracting.

The CES approach, whilst reflecting Management Contracting methods goes further, and advocates assigning the responsibilities of both Designer and Management Contractor to one person — the architect. By so doing, the technique provides a flexible professional service through the whole design and construction process, which is not normally realized in UK Management Contracting methods.

The specific advantage of this is the direct control of quality by selection of sub-contractors that satisfy the architect's criteria, and the direct involvement in the quality control and supervision process by the design team on site.

Flexibility is guaranteed both in sequence and speed of the various sub-contract operations, and by holding responsibility for construction financing, the architect can decide how money should be spent, or re-allocated, or indeed saved.

In effect the CES approach is similar to Construction Management, but with two important modifications:

1. The architect is not advisory to the Construction Manager, but responsible for the Construction Manager who is on the architect's staff.

2. Management contracts and sub-contracts with Works Contractors are not of a standard UK construction industry form, and are with the Construction Manager and not the Client. In principle, PSA-BMSE believes that a version of the CES approach to Construction Management will be possible on the Mary Rose Museum, and we will be willing to cooperate with this approach under CES direction. However, we believe that a considerable number of questions remain to be resolved.

Though the process of discussion on these outstanding issues has commenced, we believe that it will require further time, additional to that available for this report, to provide the completed organization and structure in which CES and PSA-BMSE, assisted by Bovis, can co-operate and jointly perform the construction management of the Mary Rose Museum.

CONCLUSION

We have reviewed the technical feasibility of the building carefully, and at first sight the design by CES appears to present many difficult problems. The construction of substantial foundations in proximity to No 3 Dock, the forming and erection process for the main arches, and control of the ship hall environment are the most obvious. During the course of our review it has become quite apparent however, that these problems are amenable to reasonable solution.

PSA-BMSE is of the view therefore, that nothing indicated in CES's preliminary design is impractical, and that the Museum building as currently conceived can be built within available technology and practice.

Considerable design development work remains, which will involve more physical investigation. The technical complexity of the remaining design, together with the sensitive historical setting of the building, suggests that this work should be completed before any form of construction is commenced. It is therefore imperative, in our view, that project development should proceed carefully in a sequential manner.

Our assessment of the CES Prime management methods indicates that the approach is wholly consistent with se-

quential project development, and in many ways complements such a process by pursuing true continuity between design and construction. We can strongly advocate any method which enhances continuity, and from our perspective the CES proposals are singularly aimed at such a target.

There is, without doubt, considerable work to be done outwith the mainstream of project design development. The programme illustration given earlier confines attention to the essential time-table for design and construction. We judge however, that a considerable number of extraneous issues still need to be resolved, not least the time required by the Client to secure financing and approve the project proposals, and to re-initiate the design process. This situation must inevitably cloud what should be a clear positive approach to design development which will, unless the issues are resolved immediately, impede the project and jeopardize the completion date of the ship hall.

We also believe that immediate steps should be taken to establish detailed

working arrangements, and organization for both design and construction. The preparation of a project execution plan, embracing all factors that influence the project, and reflecting a formal statement of the project objectives and the strategy for their attainment would, we believe, help to crystallize the many issues that remain to be concluded.

PSA-BMSE believes that the form of Prime management advocated by CES has advantages over more traditional methods of building procurement, but represents such a radical departure from traditional practice, that participants will inevitably need to co-operate to realize the ambitions of the methods. These include achieving very high quality, whilst at the same time holding cost and time to plan. In principle, PSA-BMSE believes that such methods will be possible, but recognizes that considerable detail remains to be worked out before the methods can be implemented. The Mary Rose Museum project, we feel, offers no technical impediments to such methods.

PSA-BMSE is confident in both the technical feasibility of the building as designed by CES, and the comprehensive cost plan that reflects the project proposals. So far as is possible at such an early stage of project development, we consider that the cost plan represents, at current UK cost, the building and fitting-out requirements for a Museum; we also consider that it is feasible to contain the current scope of the project within the cost plan budget estimate. The results, reported to us, of preliminary discussions carried out by both CES and the Mary Rose Trust into the question of planning approval for the project are most encouraging. It is clear nonetheless, that considerable consultation work remains on this issue, and we would advocate continued care and diligence in this area.

We therefore recommend a careful programme of discussion with the various planning approval bodies involved with the building, and that this deliberate programme should be regenerated immediately.

The conclusion was that these construction management methods, developed in California, can reasonably be translated into British practice to build the Mary Rose Museum.

Careful and sober analysis by BMSE, a division of one of the largest public procurement agencies in the UK — PSA — backed by its contractor manager Bovis, one of the largest private construction management firms in the UK, concluded that the management methods were sound and practical.

To repeat the key findings of the report: "PSA-BMSE is of the view therefore, that nothing indicated in CES's preliminary design is impractical, and that the Museum building as currently conceived can be built within available technology and practice" and "Our assessment of the CES Prime management methods indicates that the approach is wholly consistent with sequential project development, and in many ways complements such a process by pursuing true continuity between design and construction. We can strongly advocate any method which enhances continuity, and from our perspective the CES proposals are singularly aimed at such a target."

CHAPTER FIVE

SKETCHES OF A
SECOND DESIGN

A SECOND DESIGN, MODIFIED IN A FEW KEY POINTS, PAVES THE WAY TO INCREMENTAL CONSTRUCTION OF THE MUSEUM

In July 1992, when the Dockyard's major sponsor pulled back their funds, we began a process of refining a number of aspects of the Museum design — in response to concerns raised by the Trustees, and in response to discussion with the City of Portsmouth.

Changing Admiralty plans for the future of the Portsmouth Dockyard and the withdrawal of the shipping sponsor, had reduced the overall development that was likely to occur in the Dockyard, and thus made it more difficult to consider operating a restaurant on top of the Museum. This raised the possibility of the Museum existing without a restaurant on top. The Museum Trustees had for the first time, in June 1992, begun to express a new concern about the height of the building, and asked us to prepare plans which showed a lowered profile, without the restaurant on top. The City of Portsmouth Planning Officer had also just begun providing us with very useful feedback on the design, in anticipation of the planning application, and his views of the impact the building might make on the Dockyard had been communicated to us, with special reference to the Museum's height, its exterior materials, the configuration of the arches inside the Museum, and certain details of the Victory Arena.

As we shall now see these considerations led to a revised design in which we began, for the first time, to think of ways in which the Museum might be built incrementally — because of the reduction in available funds.[21]

This second design is far from being thought out at the same level as the first design. It represents three or four hundred man-hours of effort, compared with five thousand man-hours spent working out and developing the first design. Nevertheless, it is intended to give an indication of the way in which these new issues might be resolved.

---

21 It was not possible to consider these conceptual modifications within the scope of professional work going on in July 1992. Nevertheless, in the interests of providing as much information as possible for the Trustees of the Mary Rose Museum and for the public at large, the directors of CES decided to spend a modest sum of money to sketch a "second" museum design which incorporated these new points, and which, above all, dealt with the change of volume that would result from removal of the restaurant. Although it has not been possible to develop this modified second design in any great detail, the following sketches indicate some of the kinds of changes which could be made. These sketches of the second design should be viewed as further meditations on the form of the building — meditations which have not yet reached their final form. After more careful discussion and analysis, it may even turn out that the original design, possibly even including the restaurant on top, is after all the best approach to the problem. Or it may turn out that some combination of the first design and these early sketches for the second design, are best. In all versions that we contemplate, with or without these changes, the essential vision of the building remains fundamentally the same.

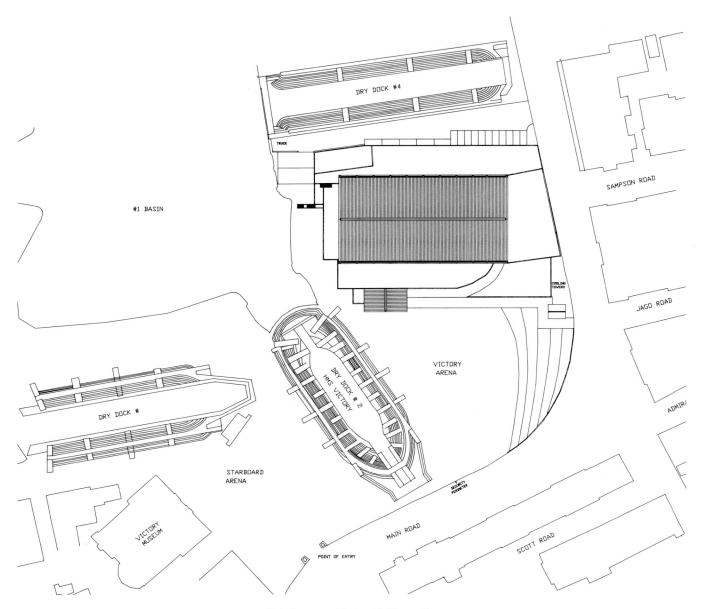

Site plan as modified, with Victory Arena

THE PLAN ITSELF IS UNCHANGED

The layout of entrance, entering ramp, museum galleries, offices, workshops, café, visitors' terraces, museum shop, access to the dock, and viewing platforms for the ship itself, are all unchanged. The plan reflects the layout arrived at in careful discussion between CES and Mary Rose Trust during 1991.

The essential functioning of the Museum is therefore unchanged, and meets all original requirements in detail.

REMOVING THE RESTAURANT

The requirement for a large restaurant in the Museum came from the original sponsor, who also intended to run the restaurant. Even at that time some

doubt had arisen about the economic feasibility of such a large restaurant, operated in this location as a "silver service" (i.e. high quality) restaurant. The location on top of the Museum was extremely tempting, and very much liked by our clients. However, uncertainty about the possibility of making this restaurant succeed financially had entered the discussion, and we had begun looking at a possible mu-

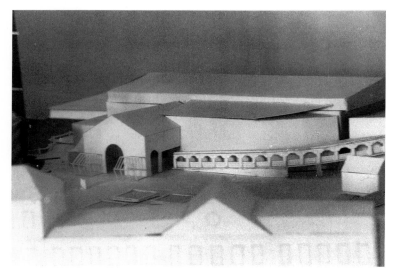

Three volume studies used to examine the effect of lowering the height of the building. From top to bottom: the 23-meter version; the 20.5-meter version; and the 16-meter version.

seum design in which there was no restaurant on top, only a large and simple roof for the ship hall itself, to enclose the dock. With the original sponsor out of the picture, the possibility of building or operating the restaurant now seemed even more remote, since an independent restaurant operator would have had to have been found. We therefore began to consider a version of the building which had no restaurant, except for the much smaller ground-floor cafe serving the museum galleries and Victory Arena.

THE NEW ROOF FORM: REDUCING THE HEIGHT OF THE BUILDING

As first designed, the roof ridge of the restaurant stood at 23 meters. In the Mary Rose Trust's June 1992 examination of the building design, they expressed for the first time some misgivings about this building height, on the grounds it might interfere with the feeling in the Dockyard, or that it might simply create political difficulties. In discussion with the Planning Officer, Les Weymes, we also found some misgivings on his side suggesting that the first design was too high and massive.

In order to accommodate the Mary Rose Trust's request for discussion of possible height reduction, we therefore made a number of studies in July 1992, in models and in drawings, to see the effect of lowering the building in various different ways. After making the models, and photographing them, we then had a lengthy discussion with the Planning Officer, in July 1992, to examine these dif-

Paper model of the second design

ferent versions. The sequence of photographs on the previous page makes the situation clear. When asked to choose one of these different volume studies, the Planning Officer chose the 20.5-meter version, the same one that we ourselves considered the most beautiful and most appropriate in height.

The chosen 20.5-meter version removes the mass at the eastern end of the building, has no restaurant, and reduces the roof ridge to a height of 20.5 meters. It appears that this version of the design completely solves the height problem — with its attendant mass and volume problems. This view was corroborated by the Planning Officer.

NEW APPROACH TO BUILDING MATERIALS AND BUILDING EXTERIOR

In another 1992 discussion with the Planning Officer, he described the depth of his concern with the overall historical and physical character of the Dockyard environment. He described his hope that the Mary Rose Museum, with the other buildings around #1 Basin, should form a harmonious whole in the character of their construction. His point of view was unusually detailed, and profoundly refreshing, in its expression of concern and in the detailed love of buildings and materials which he offered us.

He was told that we would cooperate as fully as possible with his views and his requests.

In the first design we had settled on the exterior materials of the building as some combination of concrete, brick, and tile. From CES material, and from our explanation, the Planning Officer knew that CES had, in the past, made beautiful structures with concrete, by using types of formwork and forming techniques which allow an altogether more subtle and graceful approach to detail, more reminiscent of stonework. However, even after listening to these comments, the Planning Officer asked that we look carefully at the homogeneous character of the old buildings in the

105

View of the second design, from the south, with HMS Victory on the left. In this view are we looking across the new Victory Arena, with the seats and stands on the right, and Victory's guns visible on the left foreground. The existence of the Victory Arena as the most important place in the dockyard, becomes less visible in this conception.

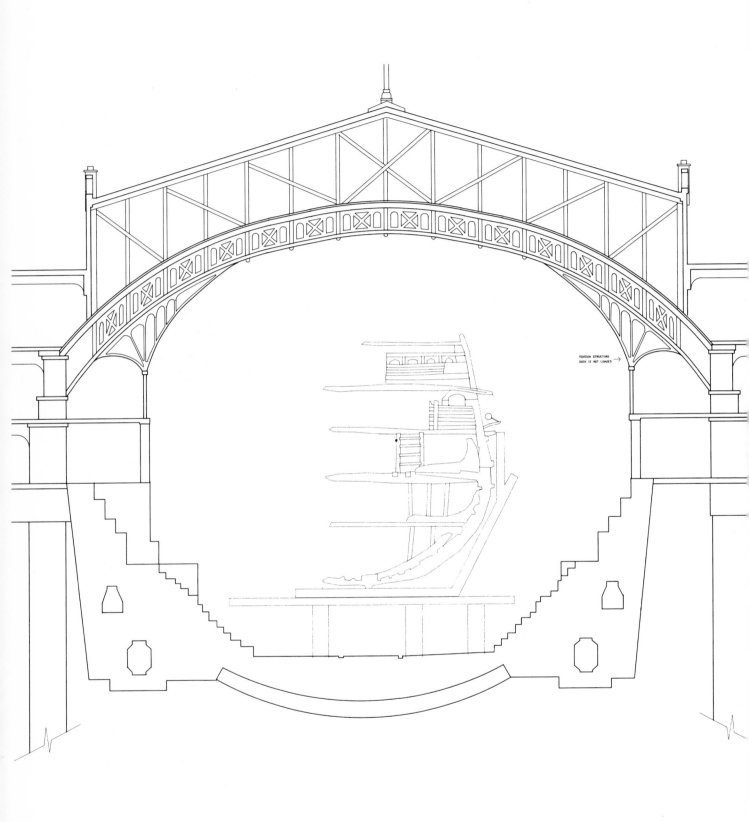

Second design. Schematic section, showing one possible approach for geometry of new structure, with reduced height. The modified arches of the ship hall. With the restaurant previously on top, removed, the great loads which inspired the first design no longer exist, and the arches are now more modest. This design of vertical parallel segments, is consistent, in feeling, with the morphology of the Tudor ship.

Dockyard. Almost every building there, virtually without exception, has a combination of brickwork, with bands of stonework. He asked, then, if it were not possible for us to consider a form of construction which would be even more harmonious with the existing use of materials and technique.

He also pointed out that cast stone is available in England, and might be used without upsetting the budget. Cast stone is a material very similar to the CES techniques of casting concrete, since it uses finer aggregates, more careful forms, and shaped forms which permit rounding, and moldings, in bands, bases, and cornices. We decided to accept the Planning Officer's advice, as far as possible, and to stick to existing Dockyard materials: brick and stone, cast stone and slate. After carefully thinking this over, we have found a version of the exterior construction which uses brick, concrete, and cast stone in a way that is directly related to the Dockyard's existing character.

The detailed treatment of brick, cast stone, tile and slate roofs is shown on the accompanying drawing. The major structure is a load-bearing wall combining brickwork and cast stone and concrete, in which the load from the arches comes down on concrete piers within the casing of the brick. The brick and cast stone are, in effect, used as formwork, for the massive concrete.

The result is visible in the intricate structure on the surface of the walls. There are stone-like panels, forming a quiet but definite pattern standing up from the surface.

The morphological character of these panels, made of

The connection between the big ship hall arches, and the small longitudinal arches spanning from pier to pier, in the second design

many repeating long and narrow rectangles, echoes the morphological character of sixteenth-century ship building and stonework.

A NEW INTERIOR STRUCTURE

In our late July meeting, the Planning Officer also told us that he had some doubt, privately, about the harmony of the great lattice arches of the first design, in relation to the ship itself, and that he felt that these arches might overshadow the ship because of their strong sense of ornament. Mary Rose Trust officers had never themselves expressed this point of view. Indeed, Margaret Rule, when we asked her about this, said that she had never been worried about the impact of the

arches on the ship, but that her own concerns about the arches, rested only on potential cleaning problems, during the conservation phase.

We began to consider the possibility that a more quiet, and more harmonious setting for the ship, might perhaps achieve the "diamond in its setting" quality, better than the lacework we had worked out for the arches in the first design. This possible change was, in some ways, the most serious of the revisions that we were contemplating. Although the first design was very strongly guided by structural considerations, and by the magnificence of the great arches and their cross-bracing, we decided that with the weight of the restaurant removed, it was possible to consider another arch system, which might be more harmoni-

Interior of the ship hall, showing revised arches

ous with the vertical lines and panels which are typical of the *Mary Rose* itself and of buildings in Tudor England.

We began work on a second arch system, with less arch depth, less cross-bracing, and a structure appropriate in total depth to the smaller load of a single roof over the ship hall. After some initial studies, this second structure has begun to achieve some sketchy structural expression.

This second structural design is however, at this stage, still very immature, and must be viewed only as an idea, not as a worked-out and coherent structure. Nevertheless, after further development, we hope that it might satisfy any critics who may share the view that the elaborate cross-bracing of the arches in the first design is too ornate. During the stage of work we

have now reached, the detailed structural design of the second design is still open, and the final "most beautiful" setting for the diamond, is perhaps yet to be found.

The accompanying drawings show the first sketches of the vision of this new structure. It is essentially a three-dimensional ribbed concrete shell, constructed in barrel vault form. The arch members themselves, at the same longitudinal spacing as before, are reduced in depth and are now only 1.7 meters deep (in the first design they were 2.4 meters deep).

THE DIMENSION OF THE ARCHES

Here we come, once again as in the first design, to the fact that the depth of the arches, and the size of their tracery plays a

critical role in the design of the ship hall.

When we began work on the second design, we knew that the loads were much less — no restaurant on top — and we knew, therefore, that the arch would not need the same depth. The arches on the first design were 2.4 meters deep at the head of the arch, and this dimension gets even bigger towards the outside as the arch splays. It is the beautiful size and proportion of this large arch, in relation to the size of the volume in the ship hall, that makes the arch help the feeling of the ship hall.

In the second design, there was no reason to have the arch as big, or as deep. A first guess as to the depth that might be needed, was 1.1 meters. We made models, and drawings, showing the arch at 1.1 meters deep. It seemed flimsy. In a later version we made it 1.2 meters. Again too flimsy. It didn't have the magnificence of the first design. Then we tried 1.5 meters. This began to work. In the section one could feel the proportions of the first ship hall gradually being recaptured. Finally, in the last series of drawings, we drew the arch with a depth of 1.7 meters. There finally it is beginning to feel right.

Why is this true? What is the justification? From a purely structural point of view, the arch certainly could be made to work with 1 or 1.1 meters. One might even say that a least-weight structure—the most so-called "efficient" structure, would be one meter deep. But at that depth the beautiful relation of the great arch, and the volume it surrounds, the wonderful volume with a boundary around it as a crowning glory—would be lost. The sense of the ship as a diamond in its setting would be lost. The sense of the relation to the natural flow of the vertical structure of columns in the galleries, in relation to the arches spanning the dock—would also be lost.

So, it was necessary to go to 1.7 meters—perhaps, one day we shall find that it has to be even more—in order to preserve the balance and harmony of the whole. It is this wholeness, in which each consideration is balanced, that defines the structure. We cannot size the arches merely by getting the efficiency of least-weight structure right. The structure has to be efficient, cheap, light in weight, set off the ship, and show a beautiful continuity with the vertical supports, and make beautifully shaped space between the arches.

Once again, doing all these things together leads in a differ-

Second design. The ceiling of the ship hall. In this design, the ceiling panels form a structural shell, stiffened by the lacework arches. The shell is made of thin reinforced concrete panels, which are cast with an embossed Tudor rose.

ent direction from an ideal of pure structural efficiency. What we are concerned with is the *overall* efficiency—the beauty—of the structure as a whole. This is more demanding, more precise, and far more complex than a numerical efficiency that can be stated only in terms of weight and force.

THE NEW POLYCHROME CEILING

In the second design, because the arches are not as deep as in the first design, the ceiling surface itself becomes more important than before. The ceiling as a whole is now functioning structurally. It is ribbed so that it functions structurally as a stiffened shell. We decided to make a virtue of this changed design, and make a beautiful ceiling hovering above the ship.

To achieve this, the ribs and stiffeners, which are made integrally with precast thin-shell concrete panels lifted into place, are now covered with polychrome. The painting on page

111

Second design: Interior of the ship hall showing the polychrome ceiling

25, and the photograph and colored drawing on these pages, show our first sketches of this polychrome. The painting on page 25 shows pale yellow arches, light crimson panels, yellow outlining and pale blue hairlines. In the center of each panel is a great, dark, Tudor rose. The colored drawing on this page shows a simpler version in red and black.

For practical reasons, the polychrome work itself should probably not be introduced until after 2020, when conservation is complete, and the ship hall has dried out. But at that stage, with the ship completely conserved, the hall open and dry, *Mary Rose* will be set off to its best by the glowing colors of the ceiling.

A MORE VIVID AND LIFE-FILLED PUBLIC SPACE NEXT TO HMS *VICTORY*

Finally, in our second design, we turned greater attention to the Victory Arena. During discussion of the first design, we had often found it difficult to get serious attention focussed on the needs of visitors in the Victory Arena — possibly because it falls between the jurisdictions of different organizations, and negotiation and politics were making it hard for any one group in the Dockyard to give this matter the full attention it deserves. However the human situation in Victory Arena is extremely important for the following reasons:

1. The place itself, being next to *Victory*, has the job of carrying the "spirit" of HMS *Victory*. The present plastic tents and booths are detrimental to this all-important emotional character.

2. In summer there are hundreds of people milling about

Second design: Ceiling panels with the Tudor rose

113

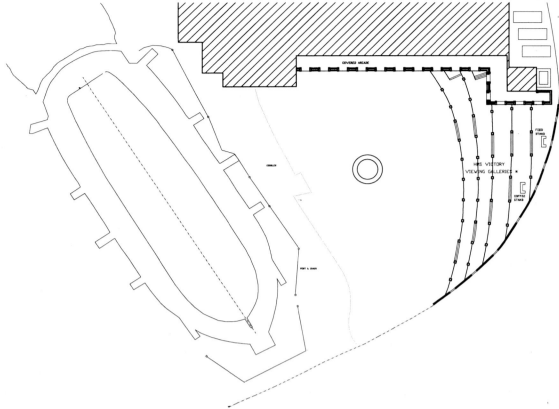

Second design: Site plan of new Victory Arena. On the right, on the east side of the arena, there are tiers of seats, facing Victory, under cover and in the shade. These seats provide a natural gathering place, provide waiting room for people visiting the museums and exhibits, and provide seating for audiences in future son-and-lumière productions or band concerts.

in this small space. This will get worse when the Mary Rose Museum is complete.

3. Also, by the time people reach this place, they may be tired, hungry, thirsty, children may be crying.

4. People desperately need a contained place where they can sit down, be protected from the bitter wind in winter, be protected from the hot sun in summer, wait to collect themselves, possibly refresh themselves with something to drink, re-group

while they wait for a ticket to HMS *Victory*, or to the *Mary Rose*.

5. It is, in many ways, the most important place in the Heritage Area. Yet it has so far barely been thought out at all.

To make the Victory Arena work practically, and come to life, we have introduced the following features into the design:

There are a great number of seats, immediately outside the Mary Rose Museum entrance, under shady cover.

There are also seats, in considerable numbers under a row of arbors, along the curve of the iron railing that separates the Arena from the Dockyard road.

In the middle of the Arena, a series of stone walls provide further seats and benches, and a place to wait.

There is a natural path which passes through the middle of the Arena and leads towards the west terrace of the Museum and the café.

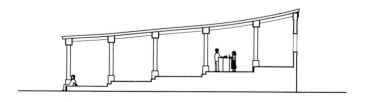

Cross section of the Victory viewing gallery

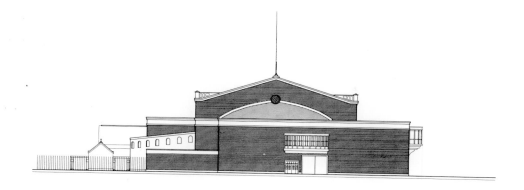

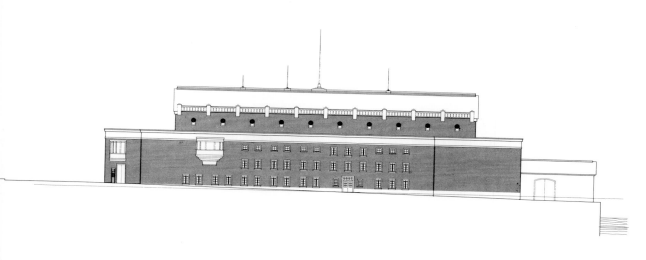

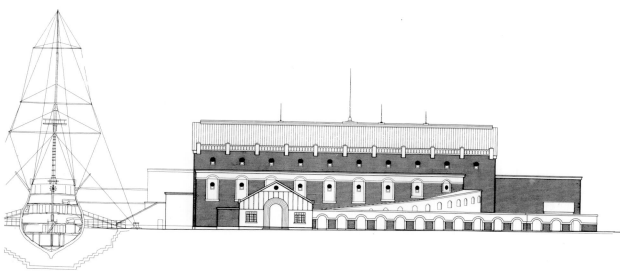

Second design of the Museum. From top to bottom: east elevation from the road;
north elevation from dry dock #4; south elevation

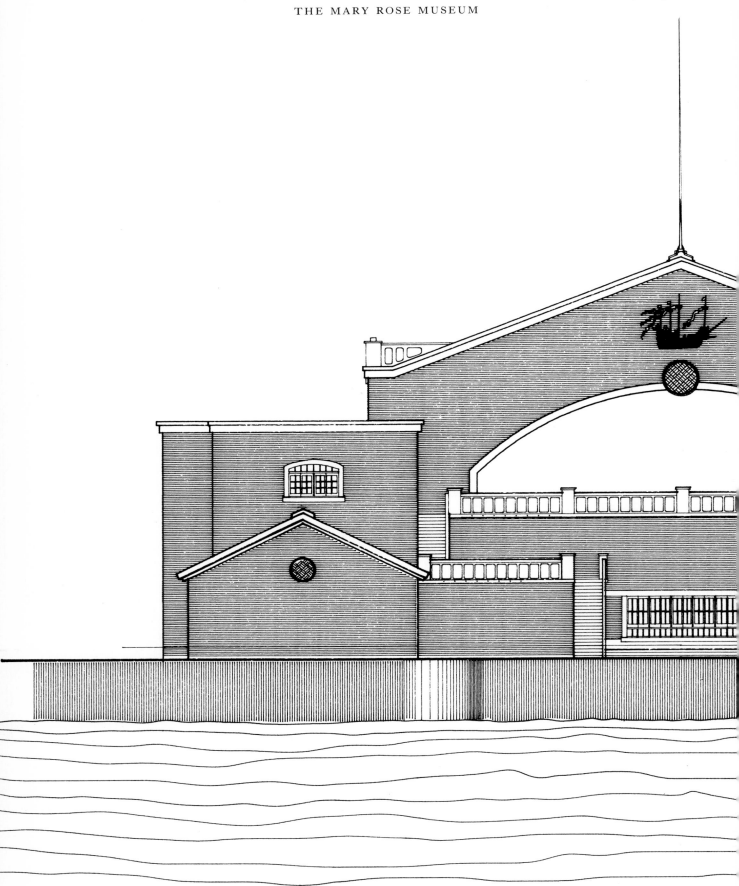

Second design: West view of the Museum, from the water

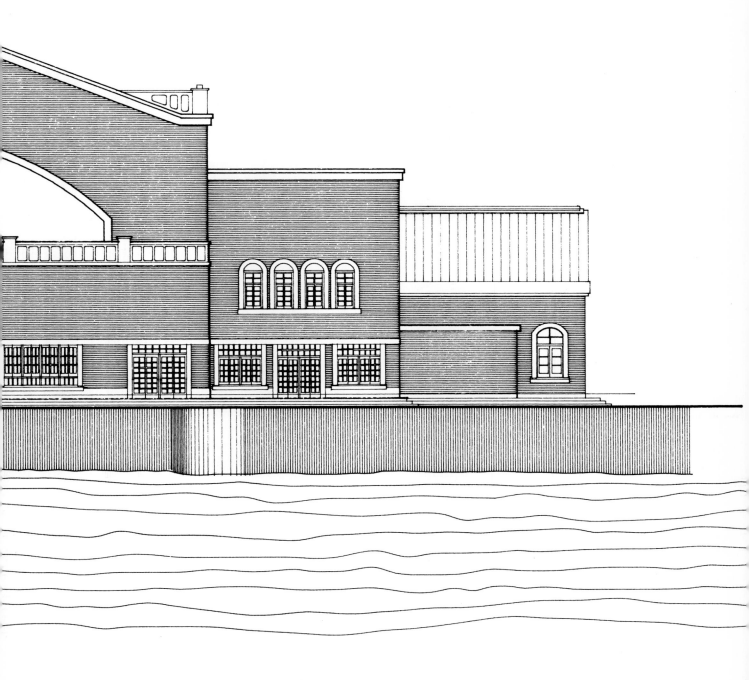

PHASED CONSTRUCTION OF THE NEW MUSEUM:
THE SHIP HALL BY ITSELF

A vital aspect of the second design concerns the phasing of construction. For financial reasons, it is very possible that the new Museum cannot now be built in a single increment of construction. The Mary Rose Trust has limited funds, and may have to build the Museum gradually with funds that are raised step-by-step over a number of years. This is not unusual. In the distant past important public buildings were often linked with fund raising, and had to be built, piecemeal, as funds became available. A museum is above all an expression of public unity, and a symbol and practical tool for confirming and elaborating our knowledge of the past. It is not, like financed construction, a money-based *development*. Thus the same pattern of action which underlay construction of the great cathedrals and country churches— the slow raising of funds, and gradual construction over time— may be perfectly appropriate for the Mary Rose Museum.

In this last section of this chapter, we show how this can be accomplished for the second design.

To solve the problems of funding, we believe the construction of the new Museum must be viewed not only as a task in architecture and building, but also as a task in money management. Since it will not necessarily be possible to find the funds for the complete Museum, all at once, we have supplemented the second design with a contingency plan which shows how the Museum can be built, step-by-step, as funds become available— while still taking care of the preservation of the ship.

Towards the end of 1992, after the loss of the Dockyard's major sponsor, the Mary Rose Trust began making contingency plans for a modest temporary expedient, designed only to protect and conserve the ship for twenty years. It was first estimated that this temporary expedient, which would provide re-cladding of the existing tent with glass reinforced plastic, together with certain other temporary improvements, would cost about £2 million ($3.4 million). Recent statements by the Trust suggest that they may be able to raise as much as £4 million.[22] Plans for this temporary expedient have been drawn up, and the Trustees believe that a sum of this magnitude can be raised successfully.

In an effort to help the Trustees best apply the funds obtained from limited fund-raising schemes, CES undertook engineering studies to find out how to make better use of an available first funding package on the order of £2 million, in such a way as to provide, not a temporary tent, but a permanent structure which would stand as the first stage in an incremental program of development for the Museum. Thus for the same sum of money, as that proposed by the Trust for purely temporary facilities, CES has shown how it is possible to build the first stage of the *permanent* Museum.

The core of the museum design, both in the first design and in the second design, is of course, the ship hall. We determined that this core of the Museum—the *Mary Rose* ship hall—can be built as an independent, "stand-alone" structure for approximately £2 million.[23]

22 John Vimpany, unpublished letter to the *Sunday Telegraph*, December 4, 1992.
23 Our first estimate showed it as £2.19 million (about $3.7 million).

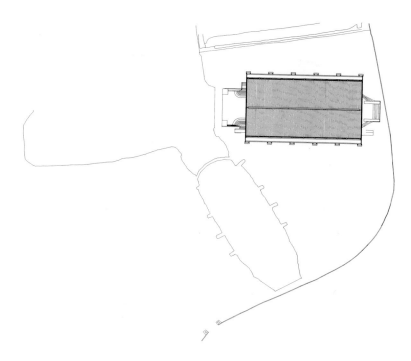

The £2 million first construction phase: Site plan

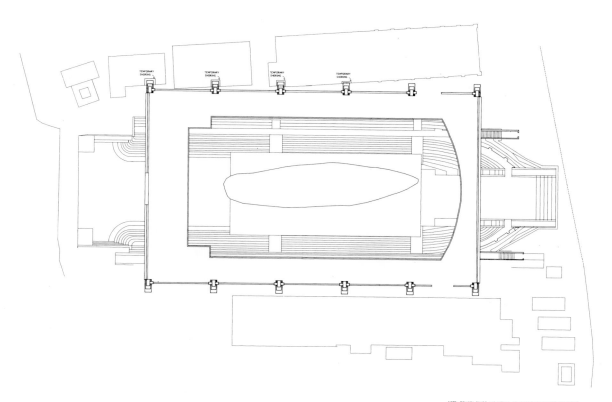

First construction phase: Ship hall ground floor plan

NOTE: COLUMN SHAPE HAS YET TO BE RECONCILED WITH COLUMN SHAPE
SHOWN ON COMPLETE MUSEUM PLANS.

119

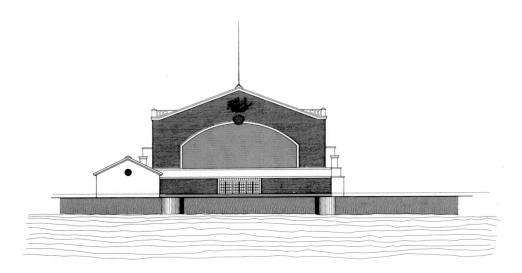

First construction phase: West elevation

This figure includes foundations, columns, arches, beams, main arches, ceiling structure with prefabricated ceiling panels, exterior walls, roof superstructure, and slate roof covering.

What is even more encouraging is that this first phase of

the Museum, which can provide the protection that the ship requires during conservation, is harmonious with the Dockyard. Thus, even in this first stage, the Museum will begin to create a necessary and harmonious atmosphere in the area around

HMS *Victory*, instead of the drab and unsuitable industrial tent now covering Dock #3.

The nature of this first-stage ship hall, and its engineering structure, includes full construction of the difficult deep-pile barrette foundations. Thus, all

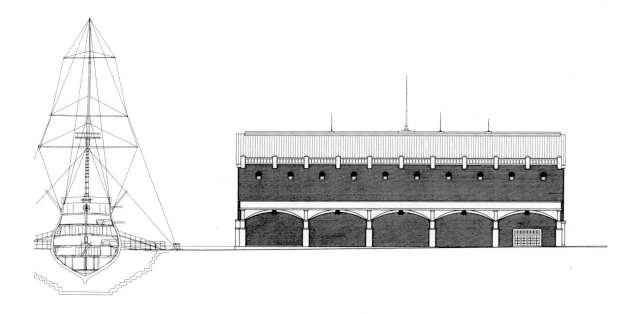

First construction phase: South elevation

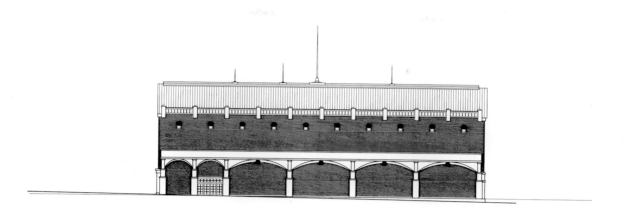

First construction phase: North elevation

subsequent structures could be added with a minimum of difficulty, and with little or no disruption to the functioning Museum. Thus, once this first stage is built the remaining parts of the Museum — museum galleries, offices, laboratories, the-

ater, shop, café, and so on — could be added incrementally, as funds become available.

It is our view that this is the most responsible use of money. Donors to the Museum will, inevitably, hope that their money is used wisely.

By comparison, the Mary Rose Trust's present proposed course of re-cladding the tent is probably not the most efficient use of money. The tent re-cladding is expensive and inefficient. And, above all, it is essentially wasteful. Money spent re-clad-

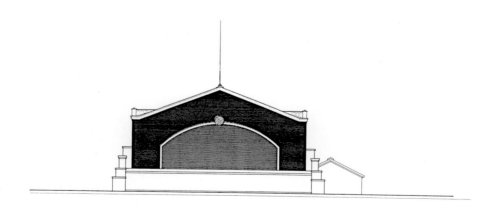

First construction phase: East elevation

121

ding the tent, must inevitably be wasted since the re-clad tent will be torn down anyway after thirty years. Meanwhile the tent, clad in grey plastic, does nothing to enhance the Dockyard, or the precious Heritage Area, for the next thirty years.

The argument has been put forward in some quarters that the ship's conservation needs require this purely technical solution in the short run, and that a proper museum cannot be built until the work of conservation is finished. This argument is surely spurious. The Museum has been designed—from the beginning—as a conservation workshop.

More important, it has been designed in such a way that it can be built over the existing tent, and the tent then removed, *at any stage of the conservation process, and without hindering or interrupting the conservation process in any way whatsoever.* Whatever funds can be gathered, should in our view be put, incrementally, towards the construction of the permanent Museum. Any other course involves waste of public and donated funds.

The fact that something permanent and valuable can be built for the Museum for the modest sum of £2 million, places the future of the Museum on a very solid basis. In addition, we believe that it will inspire people—sponsors and visitors alike—to keep the Museum growing.

It is our firm conviction that once the ship hall with its great arches is built, once people experience the *Mary Rose* in the interior of the hall, and see the beautiful exterior volume of the Museum, the impetus for the remainder of the Museum construction will soon be found.

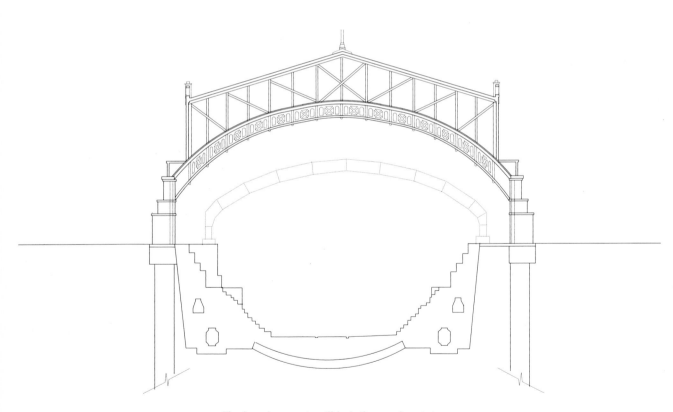

The first phase, as it will be built over the existing tent

THE LARGER
MEANING OF THE
MARY ROSE MUSEUM

PROPER CONSTRUCTION OF THE MUSEUM HAS THE POTENTIAL
TO PROVIDE A SMALL STEP IN THE EVOLUTION OF A NEW
ERA FOR BUILDING AND ARCHITECTURE

The Mary Rose Museum could become a small step in the birth of a new age in which technology and human feeling go hand in hand.

The world is waiting for a new era of common sense in respect for nature, preservation of the natural habitat, and in respect for human feeling. There is every chance that as the second millennium opens, this millennium will be remembered as the time when the first level of industrialization and mass production — which had done so much to create progress, and which had yet, at the same time, done so much to damage harmony, human feeling, and respect for nature and for life — is finally reconciled with human feeling.

The profound concern which has been expressed by many people, repeatedly, for these matters — and the profound concern expressed by the Prince of Wales — creates the hope for an era in which these concerns for nature, and for life in buildings, are finally put into practice.

The Mary Rose Museum is not a huge building. By contemporary standards it is only intermediate in size.

And yet, the ship *Mary Rose* has become a symbol of some kind — perhaps, in some degree, a symbol of that time, just before the age of rationalism, when art and architecture had

their last great moment, before the long slide towards the practical chaos of twentieth-century building.

It is fitting that this ship, which draws more than half a million visitors each year, may in its surroundings provide a vision of the future, a small monument to that enduring expression of human feeling which has tended to exist in the buildings of the past, and which has been so greatly damaged, even lost, in the architecture of our own time.

A new Mary Rose Museum, ushering in a period of greater concern with craft, an era in which the sophisticated technology of our time, and concern for spiritual comfort, go hand in hand to show how a new architecture of the twenty-first century might begin.

It is significant that this building represents a marriage of feeling and technology. It is not only rooted in a humane conception of architecture, tied closely to ordinary feeling. It is, also, an expression of engineering, a daring form of new construction. The concrete arches and trusses of this building, its innovative foundations, and the combination of these technical

achievements with a rootedness in feeling, is something new. This combination existed as a matter of course in the fifteenth century. But it has not yet existed, profoundly, in our era.

During the last twenty years, and in varying degrees, the Center for Environmental Structure has been working continuously for the kind of architecture which is described in this book. This fight began with the publication of A PATTERN LANGUAGE[24] — a rather straightforward and innocent compendium of a few hundred of the abstract structures needed, in buildings, to create human comfort. Although this material was widely acknowledged and accepted in the 1970s, some architects went out of their way to discredit it. They did this, perhaps, because even in that innocent book, there was a hint that *everything* in architecture might have to change in response to common sense. Now, eighteen years later, the factual contents of that book are more or less accepted worldwide.

The work continues today in the area of processes, already alluded to in Chapter 4. When one examines the nature of a healthy human environment

24 Christopher Alexander, S. Ishikawa, M. Silverstein, M. Jacobson, I. Fiksdahl-King, S. Angel, A PATTERN LANGUAGE, Oxford University Press, New York, 1977.

from a fundamental theoretical point of view, *it turns out that the processes through which the environment is produced in the end play the most fundamental role of all*. By processes, we mean the actual means of implementation, the role of control in designing, planning, and building, the role of money, the role of users and their needs, the sequence in design and construction, the organization of jobs by subcontractors, the management of the building process. The essence of the problem of building a structure which is profound, beautiful—in tune with human feelings and human needs—is related to adaptational problems in biology. Just as the adaptation of an organism to its environment depends on the processes by which the organism is made, grows, and so forth—so the possibility of proper, and sufficiently subtle adaptation between the building and its environment, or the building and its users—*requires* forms of control which are entirely different from the control typically exercised by big-time building managers of the modern era.

With the construction of the Mary Rose Museum as we have envisaged it, and with a combined achievement in technical mastery and in artistic feeling, there is an opportunity to show the world what architecture in the twenty-first century might really mean.

It may serve as a symbol, too, in which a new enlightenment and an awareness of human feeling—even in the details of a building—may lead the way once more to an era in which the great constructions of the past might now be joined by a new age of great constructions, once more harmonious with the earth, once more harmonious with their own engineering structure, once more harmonious with the feelings and the wishes of ordinary people everywhere.

WE HOPE

THE MUSEUM WILL ONE DAY BE BUILT

AS IT SHOULD BE BUILT